"Ours" Jesuit Portraits

M.-C. Durkin

ÉDITIONS
DU SIGNE

Acknowledgments

The author expresses warm appreciation to the following, who have been generous in contributing their ideas, time, knowledge and resources:

Rev. José M. de Vera, S.J., Director, Society of Jesus Press and Information Office, Rome
Rev. Francis Daly, S.J.
Rev. Thomas Lucas, S.J.
Mr. Martin McHugh and *Company* magazine
Rev. John Padberg, S.J., Director, Institute of Jesuit Sources, St. Louis, Missouri
Rev. Joseph N. Tylenda, S.J.

Further appreciation is due to others who have been helpful in a variety of ways, large and small, especially to

Jesuit friends and Jesuits at large, whose responses and suggestions have been invaluable
Ms. Anne Pearce, Director, The Greenlease Gallery, Rockhurst College
Dr. Jeffrey Chipps Smith
Staff at Xavier University Library, Cincinnati, Ohio
Students at St. Xavier High School and at Xavier University, Cincinnati, Ohio, who read portions of the text and made recommendations

A.M.D.G.

Published by
Éditions du Signe
BP 94 – 67038 Strasbourg – Cedex 2 – France
Tel (++33) 3 88 78 91 91
Fax (++33) 3 88 78 91 99
info@editionsdusigne.fr

Publishing Director
Christian Riehl

Director of Publication
Joëlle Bernhard

Publishing Assistant
Audrey Gilger

Layout by
Cirrus en Campagne

Photoengraving
Atelier l'engrenage
Atelier du Signe (106698)

© Éditions du Signe 2006
ISBN 10: 2-7468-1484-6
ISBN 13: 978-2-7468-1484-4

Façade design for the Church of the Gesù, Rome, by Giacomo della Porta. (Courtesy of Society of Jesus Office of Press and Information)

Front cover and page 3 (detail):
Jesus, Eternal King, Dead and Resurrected for His Company *by Sandro Arduini (1991) at the University of Prayer, L'Aquila, Italy (Yearbook S.J. 2003, Courtesy of Society of Jesus Office of Press and Information)*

Front cover background
(Courtesy of the Institute of Jesuit Sources)

Back cover (from left to right; top to bottom:
Ignatius Loyola (Frontispiece, Life of Ignatius *published by Barbé, 1609)*
Eusebio Kino (Sculpture in Tucson by Julián Martínez, photo by Godehard Bruentrup, S.J.)
John Courtney Murray (Courtesy of New York Province Archives)
Pope Benedict XVI and Father General Peter-Hans Kolvenbach (Courtesy of Society of Jesus Office of Press and Information)
Peter Faber (Courtesy of the Institute of Jesuit Sources)
Francis Xavier (By Salaverría, in Palacio de Navarra, Pamplona)
Mexican seminarians at Los Gatos, California, 1915, with Miguel Pro in the back row, second from left. (Courtesy of California Province Jesuit Archives)

Introduction

We say that variety is the spice of life. If so, then the Jesuits portrayed in the following pages have surely added spice, zest, originality, interest, color to the life of the Society of Jesus. To start at the beginning, who could have imagined three more disparate characters than the first three among the ten companions/founders of the Jesuits, Ignatius of Loyola, Francis Xavier and Peter Faber, or three more different ways of living out the life and carrying out the mission of the Society of Jesus?

"Ours": Jesuit Portraits fully lives up to the promise inherent in the stories of those first three of "Ours" (a shorthand Jesuit term for fellow members of the Society).

To mention only a few contrasting examples from among the many in these pages: How different in background, training and response to God's call were such men as Edmund Campion, Oxford scholar and English martyr; Aloysius Gonzaga, Italian Renaissance nobleman and hero of service to the plague stricken; Matthew Ricci, sympathetic interpreter of Christianity and China to each other; and Isaac Jogues and John de Brébeuf, missionaries and martyrs among the Huron and Iroquois tribes of North America!

How different, also, were two theologians, Robert Bellarmine of the sixteenth and seventeenth centuries and Karl Rahner of the twentieth, but both advancing our understanding of God and church by "doing the truth in love," as St. Paul says, and both sometimes suffering for it in the incomprehension of highly placed churchmen! What contrast in the lives of Antonio Ruiz de Montoya, who worked in the jungles of Paraguay in the seventeenth century, and Gerard Manley Hopkins, a nineteenth-century Jesuit and one of the great poets of the English language! Peter DeSmet, among the best known Jesuits of the nineteenth century in his work among Native Americans, and Rupert Mayer, the German who courageously confronted the Nazis in the 1930s and 40s, were Jesuits in vastly dissimilar circumstances. Costanzo Beschi, the "Father of Tamil prose" in India, and Roger Boscovich, multi-talented scientist, further manifest that variety.

Finally, Pedro Arrupe, a superior general of the Society, was a champion of renewal in the church, and Rutilio Grande in Central America and João de Deus Gonçalves Kamtedza in Africa were martyrs of solidarity with the poor.

These are only a few of the men and their extraordinary stories in this fascinating and informative book that, century by century from the sixteenth to the twenty-first, not only sketches them as persons but situates them vividly in the circumstances of their times.

Why did these Jesuits live and act as they did? St. Ignatius put it very briefly as *ayudar las almas*, translated "to help souls," but *almas* really means "whole persons." They wanted to bring the men and women of their times and places to a knowledge and love of Jesus Christ and to a loving service of each other both in the community of the church and, more inclusively, in the whole world. They wanted to help toward "a world at once more human and divine," in the words of the Thirty-second General Congregation (general meeting of Jesuits officially representing their world-wide brethren) in 1974-75. Over 450 years "Ours" portrayed here were "servants of Christ's mission," to use the words of the Thirty-fourth General Congregation (1995), to help all men and women in the great human family to be, in all their variety, all that God lovingly wants them to be.

John W. Padberg, S.J.
Director
The Institute of Jesuit Sources

■ *Ignatius is ready to set out on mission. This detail of a sculpture group designed by Juan M. García de Alba, S.J., and cast by Pedro Jiménez is in the Puenta Grande retreat center in Mexico. (Yearbook S.J. 2001, courtesy of Society of Jesus Office of Press and Information)*

TABLE OF CONTENTS

TRIPTYCH:
LOYOLA, FABER, XAVIER

"...what helps most...must be...the interior law of charity and love which the Holy Spirit writes and engraves upon hearts...." (Ignatius Loyola)

Ignatius Loyola

Peter Faber

Francis Xavier

Triptych: Loyola, Xavier, Faber

■ *Ignatius Loyola by Jacopino del Conte*
(Courtesy of the Institute of Jesuit Sources)

Three college roommates. Three great men. Three holy companions: Ignatius Loyola, Francis Xavier, Peter Faber.

At the College of St. Barbe in Paris, "We shared our room, our means and our purse," Faber recounted. In the depths of his own heart each man answered God's call. In companionship they unfolded the meaning of that call. They cast aside all other ambitions, left homes and countries behind and bound themselves to Christ and to one another in the Society of Jesus.

God's work dispersed them across the face of the earth. "We must be pilgrims," wrote Xavier, "ready to go wherever we can to serve God our Lord more." Ignatius served God in Rome as the stable center that held the expanding Society together.

"Like this, Francis? Like this?" Ignatius cried, with a father's concern. He was checking Xavier's worn garments to be sure that the great missionary would depart for Asia with warm clothes. They would never see each other again, but their letters reveal their affectionate longing for a reunion.

A mission of spiritual transformation kept Faber on the move in Europe, from country to country, often on foot, always in obedience to the needs of the Church and the Society.

Both Xavier and Faber set out before the Society of Jesus had been formally instituted; both made their vows in their mission fields, Xavier in India and Faber in Germany. United with Ignatius even at great distances, these men set the stamp of their zeal on the new Society through evangelization and spiritual direction.

■ *Francis Xavier*
(Statue by Professor Bernard Schmidt, photo by Greg Rust, used by permission of Xavier University, Cincinnati)

■ *Peter Faber*
(Courtesy of the Institute of Jesuit Sources)

■ *Page 7: Ignatius and Faber courtesy of the Institute of Jesuit Sources, Xavier by Salaverría*

A Time of Transitions
The Founding Moment

Born into feudalism, the first Jesuits absorbed its medieval culture of loyalty and honor. Yet history propelled them into a rapidly expanding and fractured world, the true beginnings of modern times.

Theirs was a time of transition. The Europe of the past had seemed self-contained and to some extent unified. Most wars involved dynastic rivalries. Europe's unifying principle had been the Catholic Church, which had provided institutions of governance, communication and education as well as an understanding of humanity's ultimate purpose and how to achieve it. When challenged, this unity was sometimes harshly enforced; for example, the Inquisition investigated and punished deviations from accepted teachings.

Ignatius Loyola, Francis Xavier and Peter Faber entered adulthood as the discoveries of Columbus and other navigators were challenging long-held ideas. Europe was no longer alone in the world. And it was no longer one Europe, but a seething pot in which nations took form, often in warfare. Humanism rediscovered ancient "pagan" culture. Science was opening unimagined frontiers, understanding the world in new terms. Older theories no longer seemed adequate, but new ideas met resistance.

Festering problems within the Church cried out for reform. Many Catholics found that religious practices failed to nourish their relationship with God. Some reformers, like Luther and Calvin, formed new faith communities with their protesting followers. Others sought to make the needed changes within the Church.

The changing times fragmented Europe and the Catholic Church. Only a builder with deep, strong foundations and keen forward vision could bridge the chasms.

■ *A medieval spirit lingered in sixteenth-century Spain, as much of Western Europe experienced the new developments of the Renaissance and Protestant Reformation. (Mural by Paulo Porcella, S.J., at UNISINOS, Brazil)*

In Paris, Ignatius Loyola gathered other students into spiritual companionship. (This engraving is one of a series on the life of Ignatius, many of which were designed by the great Flemish artist Peter Paul Rubens. The collection was published by the engraver Jean Baptiste Barbé in 1609, the year Ignatius was beatified.)

A brief sketch of the Society's beginnings demonstrates how a great man, in companionship, shaped a movement that would address the needs of a new age.

Ignatius Loyola lived the transition of his epoch in his bones. Born into the Basque nobility in 1491, he spent his young manhood as a courtier. Relationships of loyalty and service to feudal lords colored his conversion experience at thirty with this worldview. He chose to serve under the standard of Christ as his lord and laid his weapons at the feet of Mary, in a ritual akin to knighthood. Then he undertook the supreme spiritual activity of the Middle Ages, a pilgrimage to the Holy Land.

His zeal "to help souls" led Ignatius to the University of Paris in 1528. Education would be a tool of his apostolate. He studied and counseled others, including his roommates Francis Xavier and Peter Faber. Two young Spaniards, Diego Laínez and Alfonso Salmerón, joined their companionship, followed by Spaniard Nicolás de Bobadilla and Portuguese Simão Rodrigues.

These seven "friends in the Lord" gathered regularly for potluck suppers, prayer and spiritual conversation. They decided to go to Jerusalem, to "spend their lives there helping souls." If that were not possible, they would go to Rome and undertake whatever ministries the Pope thought to be "for the greater glory of God [ad majorem Dei gloriam] and the good of souls."

On the feast of Mary's Assumption, August 15, 1534, Faber celebrated Mass in the Chapel of the Martyrs on Montmartre, and the companions vowed to carry out their purpose and to live in poverty and in celibate chastity.

Finishing their education was a high priority, so that they might serve better. They regrouped in Italy in 1537. They had added Claude Jay, Jean Codure, Paschase Broët and Diego Hoces (died 1538). In June, Ignatius and the others not previously ordained became priests.

Weather and warfare ruled out a voyage to Jerusalem that year. Instead, the companions volunteered in hospitals. They nursed patients, heard confessions, scrubbed floors, buried the dead. They begged for their meager food. They preached in public piazzas, gathering an audience by shouting and waving their hats. They were "helping souls" through the works of mercy. They called themselves the "Company of Jesus," companions of Christ, companions in his service.

The Society first made its home at a church honoring Mary as the Madonna della Strada, "Our Lady of the Way." This fresco was later incorporated into the Church of the Gesù. (Courtesy of the Institute of Jesuit Sources)

The early Society caught the missionary spirit of Ignatius captured in this statue in Uruguay. (Yearbook S.J. 2001, photo courtesy of the Society of Jesus Office of Press and Information)

In Rome, they placed themselves at the service of the Church in the person of Pope Paul III. The Pope sent Faber and Laynez to teach theology at the University of Rome, while Ignatius devoted himself to spiritual guidance. The companions heard confessions, preached and began Christian instruction for boys. New members, all highly educated, joined them. Assisted by benefactors, they established a residence for Jewish converts, one for former prostitutes and another for orphans. They settled near the urban church of Santa Maria della Strada (Mary of the Street).

Despite some opposition, the Society of Jesus received official Church approval in September 1540. The Society was already meeting global needs, as Portuguese and Spanish rulers recruited these preachers as missionaries for Asia and the Americas. Jesuit schools and colleges sprang up, providing Christian education for clergy and lay men, meeting intellectual and spiritual needs and contributing to Church renewal. When Ignatius died in 1556, there were over fifty colleges in Europe, India and Brazil.

By that time there were also 1000 Jesuits, preaching, teaching and evangelizing across Europe, as far east as Japan and as far west as Brazil. One man's response to God had built this bridge into a new world.

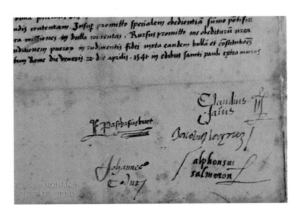

The companions present in Rome signed the document of their vows in the new Society of Jesus April 22, 1541. (Photo by Thomas Lucas, S.J.)

The First Companions

With Ignatius, Xavier and Faber, seven more Companions gathered as the Company of Jesus in Italy in 1537.

■ Diego Laynez (1512 –1565)

Diego Laynez arrived in Paris from Spain in 1533. As he dismounted at an inn, Ignatius Loyola was on hand. Soon Laynez shared the companions' commitment to God and one another at Montmartre.

Laynez both preached and lectured widely for the masses. His impact as a theologian at the Council of Trent overcame the prejudices he encountered on account of his Jewish ancestry and shabby dress.

Elected the second superior general in 1558, Laynez dealt with challenges to the Society's apostolic nature. He was trusting of his men, loving and lovable. Asthma, malaria and exhaustion struck him down in 1565.

■ Alfonso Salmerón (1515-1585)

Alfonso Salmerón of Toledo was eighteen and eager to learn when he arrived in Paris with his friend Laynez. Both dedicated themselves at Montmartre in 1534.

Among his apostolic works in several countries, he spoke as a papal theologian at the Council of Trent and represented Pope Paul III on an unsuccessful mission to Ireland. After serving as provincial of Naples, he wrote voluminously.

■ Nicolás de Bobadilla (1509-1590)

From Palencia, Spain, Nicolás de Bobadilla joined the founding group. He would later write to these companions almost weekly, yet he accused Ignatius of tyranny and opposed Laynez at the papal court. He hobnobbed with rulers but also challenged them boldly; Emperor Charles V once had him kidnapped.

Unwilling to settle down, he was a military chaplain in Africa, then crisscrossed Italy on his white horse, preaching effectively and reforming monasteries and dioceses, invited by bishops and princes. He outlived all the other original companions.

■ Simão Rodrigues (1513-1579)

The Portuguese Simão Rodrigues opened his heart to Ignatius in 1533 and joined the band of spiritual friends. Rodrigues was to go to India with Xavier but was reassigned to Lisbon. He became the first provincial of Portugal. He tutored the king's son and seemed excessively fond of court life. When Ignatius sent him to Spain, he balked and was nearly expelled from the Society. He founded Jesuit schools at Évora and Coimbra, marked by a religious extremism that mirrored his own weakness in common sense.

■ Claude Jay (ca. 1500-1552)

Peter Faber's Savoyard schoolmate Claude Jay was a priest, conducting a small school, when Faber encouraged him in 1533 to study in Paris. Faber directed him in the Spiritual Exercises, and Jay joined the group in 1535.

Jay worked in Italy and in Germany and founded a college in Vienna. He attended the Council of Trent and the Diet of Augsburg.

■ Paschase Broët (1500-1562)

The priest Paschase Broët of Picardy made the Exercises with Faber and joined the companions in 1536.

In the Society, he labored in Italy and was sent on the unsuccessful mission to Ireland. He was the provincial of France and died in Paris while serving the victims of plague.

■ Jean Codure (1508-1541)

Jean Codure of Provence was studying theology when he met Faber. He joined the companions in 1536. Ordained in Venice in 1537, he died in 1541.

■ Diego Hoces (1490-1538)

Meeting Ignatius in Venice, Diego Hoces made the Exercises with him in 1537. He died unexpectedly in 1538.

Chapter I · Triptych: Loyola, Xavier, Faber · **13**

Loyola Castle at Azpeitia in the Basque province of Guizpúzcoa, Spain, was the Loyola ancestral home. (Photo by Don Doll, S.J., courtesy of the Institute of Jesuit Sources)

Ignatius Loyola (1491-1556)

(Photo by Thomas Lucas, S.J.)

A threadbare pilgrim limped across the face of Europe, into the heart of humanity.

He had laid aside his sword and dagger. He had left the courtier's luxuries and social-climbing. He was traveling to God and to the whole world.

Iñigo López de Loyola had enjoyed a life befitting his birth in a castle of the Basque country's minor nobility in 1491. After very basic schooling, his education concentrated on courtly manners, dress and politics. In his teens and early twenties, he polished these skills among the nobility and in Spain's royal court. He first served in the retinue of Juan Velázquez de Cuéllar, King Ferdinand's treasurer, then in that of the duke of Nájera.

Vain about his appearance, Iñigo liked the figure he cut in the era's fashionable tight stockings. He was proud of his "fine head of hair." Drinking, carousing and sexual transgressions were a part of his world, and he took part in them all. Religion formed a backdrop but meant little to him.

As the thirteenth child, he had to win his way in a feudal world. In the duke's service, he found himself on the battlements of Pamplona when it was besieged by French soldiers on May 20, 1521. Leadership and heroic ideals were second nature to Iñigo. He persuaded his comrades to mount a defense of the Spanish garrison. The French cannon took up bombardment positions; fired. Missiles sped over the citadel wall. One found its mark, shattering Iñigo's right leg. With their leader fallen, the Spanish surrendered immediately. Iñigo de Loyola's brief career as a soldier came to an end. He did not guess that the disaster had opened a door.

Ignatius later described himself in youth as "given over to vanities of the world." He liked the way he looked as a courtier. This copy of a painting by Titian hangs in the Gesù residence, Rome. (Photo courtesy of Thomas Lucas, S.J.)

Back home in the Loyola castle, Iñigo faced surgery—"butchery," he called it. Doctors told him to prepare for death on June 28, the eve of the feast of Saints Peter and Paul. Iñigo had a devotion to Peter, the action-prone leader of the Apostles, and prayed especially to him. By midnight he had turned the corner. He would live.

During a long recuperation, Iñigo read and thought and was open to God's grace. (Engraving attributed to Cornelius Galle the Elder, in Life of Ignatius published by Barbé, 1609)

When the doctors finished their work, his leg was deformed. He demanded further surgery to remove an ugly lump, thinking of his appearance in stylish clothes. With intense pain, he paid the price of his vanity. Then followed the torture of stretching the leg to the length of the other. Yet he would always limp.

What was a bored man of action to do in a long, lonely recuperation? Iñigo enjoyed reading fiction, especially romantic tales about knights, but the castle had no such books. In desperation he leafed through a life of Christ and the lives of the saints. He actually began to admire their heroic deeds of holiness and imagined himself outdoing the saints. In another sort of daydream, he spent hours thinking about "a certain lady," about how he would win her love with poetry, romantic speeches and deeds of valor.

Solitude was nourishing a hidden gift that Iñigo had never cultivated, interior insight. He began to recognize that the two kinds of imaginings produced different responses. Worldly thoughts gave him passing pleasure, while spiritual thoughts led to more lasting happiness. He decided to imitate the saints.

Iñigo's bedroom is now the Conversion Chapel (Courtesy of the Institute of Jesuit Sources)

As a casualty of war, Iñigo endured excruciating wounds and surgeries. This detail of a sculpture group designed by Juan M. García de Alba, S.J., and cast by Pedro Jiménez is in the Puenta Grande retreat center in Mexico. (Yearbook S.J. 2001, courtesy of Society of Jesus Office of Press and Information)

The Pilgrim set out first for the shrine of Our Lady
at the Benedictine abbey of Montserrat in Catalonia,
a trip of over 300 miles. (Ceiling Fresco by Andrea Pozzo, S.J.,
photo by Thomas Lucas, S.J.)

At the Benedictine monastery of Montserrat,
he kept vigil before the venerable statue of the
Black Madonna. At her feet he laid his sword and
dagger. The next morning, in clothing made of a
sack-like fabric "loosely woven and very prickly,"
he took up his staff and water gourd and was on
his way, a pilgrim bound for Jerusalem.

In the small town of Manresa, the Pilgrim spent nearly
a year in intense prayer and penance, begging alms
and experiencing God's deep inner guidance. (Photo by
Don Doll, courtesy of the Institute of Jesuit Sources)

Early in his
pilgrimage, Iñigo
began to keep a
spiritual journal.
(Photo by Thomas
Lucas, S.J.)

His next stop was Manresa, near Barcelona,
where he spent almost a year. Iñigo threw himself
into extreme penances. Mood swings plagued
him. Remorse for his past sins tormented him. Yet
inner consolation also flowed from his mystic
experiences. With his "interior eyes," he saw
Christ's humanity in a brilliant but indistinct
bodily form. He saw the Trinity symbolized by
three keys of an organ.

Before Mary's altar,
the Pilgrim laid his
weapons and kept an
all-night vigil. This
bas relief is one of
a series at Manresa,
depicting Ignatius's
conversion experience.

He contemplated God's love creating and
redeeming him and continuing to work in his life.
Attention to God's guidance formed the basis for
notes that developed into the Spiritual Exercises.
The former soldier enlisted under the banner of
"Christ the Lord, the Eternal King."

Iñigo had discovered the secret of a meaningful
life: union with God and service to others,
"helping souls." Begging and sleeping in
doorways, he made his way to Jerusalem, hoping
to serve there. However, the religious authorities
would not allow him to stay. Iñigo recognized that
God was teaching him through this disappointment.

*Ex Oliueto reuertens ab Armenio custode voce,
ac fuste terretur; dumq ne solitarius ea loca pera-
graret, ferociter in hospitium trahitur, inter ea con-
uicia, et contumelias Christum aspicit praeeuntem.*

The Pilgrim arrived in Jerusalem in September, 1523.
Here he is punished for disobedience. (Engraving from Life
of Ignatius, published by Barbé, 1609)

Ignatius was helping these men to pay attention to the Holy Spirit at work in their own souls. The three began the spiritual companionship that drew four others into their circle and was confirmed by vow on Montmartre in 1534. While making the Exercises, each man committed himself to God's service.

Compluti primum ; postea Salmanticæ, calumnias pro Christo, et carcerem passus, ex ipso etiam carcere animas lucratur, magnoq. spiritus feruore succensus. Non tot, inquit, in hac vrbe sunt compedes, quin plures ego Christi causa percupiam. 36

Though imprisoned by the Inquisition in Alcalá, Iñigo continued his ministry of helping souls, as people still sought him out behind bars. (Engraving attributed to Cornelius Galle the Elder, in Life of Ignatius *published by Barbé, 1609)*

Back in Spain he taught religion in the streets in Alcalá. No one could ignore this man's intense connection with God, and companions joined him. Rumors about these "sack-wearers" reached the ears of the Inquisition in 1527, and he was arrested. Were they a sect? Had Iñigo led women astray? After forty-two days in jail, the verdict was "not guilty." He was released with a warning not to "speak [publicly] about matters of faith until [he] had studied four more years."

Alone, on foot, he braved the seven-hundred-mile trek through war-torn regions to the University of Paris. There Ignatius (Latin name which he adopted) roomed with two younger students, Peter Faber and Francis Xavier. Faber had long wanted to be a priest, but he was doubting his vocation. Directed by Ignatius in the Spiritual Exercises, he found peace. Xavier resisted his roommate's influence at first. At last, he too chose to serve God.

The Spiritual Exercises

Ignatius kept notes about his intense experience of God at Manresa in 1522/23. These formed the basis of The Spiritual Exercises, a program for a spiritual retreat. The notes guide the director in leading a retreatant through four weeks of prayer and contemplation.

The Exercises use memory, imagination, mind and heart with astute insight into human nature. They teach methods of prayer and discernment in making choices. They lead the participant through an understanding of God's love and toward a committed personal response of love. Drawing upon Ignatius's experience as a soldier, the Exercises pose a choice between enlisting under the battle flag of Christ or that of Lucifer.

Perhaps the most familiar passage in the Exercises is the self-offering often called by its first word in Latin, "Suscipe":

"Take, Lord, and receive all my liberty, my memory, my understanding, and my entire will, all that I have and possess. Thou hast given all to me. To thee, O Lord, I return it. All is Thine, dispose of it wholly according to Thy will. Give me Thy love and Thy grace, for this is sufficient for me."

The Principle and Foundation of the Exercises, including meditation on Creation and Sin, are interpreted by Brazilian muralist José M. Fernandes Machado, S.J. in the Ignacio de Azeveda Novitiate Chapel, São Paulo, Brazil. (Photo courtesy of Rodrigo Zaniolo)

While on the way to Rome, near the village of La Storta Ignatius saw Jesus carrying his cross; God the Father placed him with Jesus, who told him, "I wish you to serve us." (Anonymous, courtesy of the Society of Jesus Office of Press and Information)

Recognizing that the Jerusalem pilgrimage was impossible, Ignatius and two of the companions walked to Rome, to the center of the Church. At the village of La Storta along the way, he experienced God placing him at the side of Jesus, who said, "I wish you to serve us."

Ignatius engaged in works of mercy among Rome's poor and marginalized and guided more and more people through the Exercises, helping them to understand God's invitation in their hearts.

Official Church approval for the Society of Jesus came in September 1540. In April 1541 Ignatius was elected superior. In prayer, study and consultation he formulated the Society's Constitutions, helped by his secretary, Juan Polanco. Mystical experiences, especially at Mass, guided him.

As the Society became international, even intercontinental, the pilgrim became an administrator. His advice to Xavier must have echoed his own experience of service through his many spiritual sons: "sending others and guiding them...you will do in many places what you would have done in one by yourself." He was also a father, described as being "all love." Once, welcoming a very tall new Jesuit, the short Father General had to jump to hug him.

Negotiating royal and papal politics, developing resources for ministries, handling personnel problems, supporting the Catholic Reform.... Seven thousand letters remain of his vast correspondence. Yet he ministered personally to beggars and to nobles.

The founder finally agreed to dictate his autobiography. He spoke of the awareness of God's presence, always with him, filling those last years.

Pope Paul III gave official Church approval to the new Society of Jesus in 1540. Cardinal Alessandro Farnese (center) was later the patron of the Church of the Gesù. (Anonymous, courtesy of the Society of Jesus)

He was sixty-five when his tired body told him it was the end. He asked Polanco to beseech the Pope's blessing for him. When the secretary delayed, considering other business more pressing, Ignatius humbly replied, "Do as you think best." The doctors were not alarmed, but Brother Canizzaro reported very early on July 31, 1556, that the sick man had spent a restless night, often calling out, "Oh God!" Before 6 a.m. he was dead.

One man's experience of God, one man's journey, intersected with the spiritual needs of an age. In him the Holy Spirit catalyzed an explosion of energy that has filled the world.

Ignatius Loyola was canonized in 1622. His feast is July 31.

■ *(Courtesy of the Institute of Jesuit Sources)*

■ *"He had many visions when he said mass, and when he was drawing up the constitutions he had them with great frequency."* – The Autobiography *(Peter Paul Rubens, Flemish, 1577-1640. Saint Ignatius of Loyola, ca. 1620-22. Oil on canvas, 88" x 54 ½". [223.5 x 138.4 cm]. Norton Simon Art Foundation)*

The Formula of the Institute

■ *(Painting by José de Ribera, Courtesy of the Institute of Jesuit Sources)*

The companions prayed for enlightenment and reflected on their experience, then discussed the essence of the Society (*societas*, Latin equivalent of "company") in 1539. A brief outline, called "Five Chapters" or "Formula of the Institute," summarized their vision:

● soldiers of God devoted to "the advancement of souls...propagation of the faith by the ministry of the word, by spiritual exercises, by works of charity...by the instruction in Christianity of children and the uneducated";

● obedience to the Pope, "whether he may send us to the Turks or to the New World or to Lutherans or to others...";

● obedience to the superior in all matters related to the Society's goals and Rule of life;

● dependence on God (through the goodness of benefactors), owning no real estate or income-producing property except to educate new members (and eventually lay students);

● priority of works of charity over communal praying of the Divine Office and over intense penances; long preparation of candidates.

Peter Faber (1506-1546)

Corruption and ignorance plagued the sixteenth-century Church and divided Europe through sectarian wars. Emperor Charles V brought Catholics and Protestants into dialogue at Worms. Concerned monarchs and bishops tried to rehabilitate the local clergy. Pope Paul III called the Council of Trent to plan reforms.

Tending souls was Peter Faber's response. While others taught and preached in more public venues, Faber addressed spiritual needs privately, in personal conversations. He guided earnest seekers through the Spiritual Exercises. He heard confessions, helping penitents turn to God. He advised church and government leaders on eradicating corruption. Through the many individuals he touched, his impact was multiplied and contributed to the reformist movement that began to heal the Church.

As a young shepherd in the Alpine foothills, Peter Faber absorbed the beauty of his pastoral surroundings. Bright and religious, he would stand on a rock to preach to his playmates in the village of Villaret, Savoy. He was so lovable that both children and adults liked to listen.

Peter enjoyed learning. At ten he began lessons in a nearby village. His studies continued through his teens, until he was ready for the University of Paris in 1525.

Wrestling with conflicting urges, at twelve Peter made a promise to be chaste. Yet his powerful sexual feelings tormented and confused him. As a college student he bounced from one idea to another. Should he be a priest or monk? Be a physician, a lawyer, a teacher? Should he marry? Was he a terrible sinner? Was he better than his classmates?

Peter was such a brilliant student that his Greek teacher asked him to tutor his new roommate, Ignatius Loyola. One day he was explaining a passage in Aristotle's writings to Ignatius. Peter paused, looked up from the page and began to pour out his torments. "He helped me understand my own conscience," Peter later wrote. The result was peace of heart. Peter decided to become a priest.

Peter began to see his path; it followed the footsteps of Ignatius. "We came to be completely united in our desires and our firm resolve to take up this way of life...." The third roommate, Francis Xavier, was slower to join their resolve, but by 1533 they were all spiritual companions. When Peter made the Spiritual Exercises in early 1534, he accompanied his prayer with such severe penances, in bitter cold, that Ignatius had to teach him moderation.

On August 15, 1534, the feast of the Assumption, the newly ordained Peter Faber celebrated Mass in the Chapel of the Martyrs on Montmartre. Seven men bound themselves by vow to serve God and help souls, preferably in Jerusalem. When that destination proved impossible, they committed themselves to whatever the Pope directed.

■ *As Faber raises the host during Mass, the friends vow themselves to God on August 15, 1534, on Montmartre, Paris. (Courtesy of the Institute of Jesuit Sources)*

As the only priest among them, Peter Faber celebrated the Mass at which the first "friends in the Lord" vowed their commitment at the Chapel of the Martyrs on Montmartre, in Paris on August 15, 1534. (Engraving from Life of Ignatius published by Barbé, 1609)

For Faber, that obedience meant, first, teaching theology and Scripture in Rome's university of La Sapienza and, next, assisting the papal legate in Parma. He settled into a hospital rather than the cardinal's palace. As a confessor and spiritual director Faber had such an impact that Parma's citizens returned to the sacraments in droves, and "each Sunday looked like Easter Sunday," according to a witness.

Faber's great gift was personal guidance, in conversation and in confession. He treated all—royalty and ruffians—with firm and gentle respect. One night, lost on the road between Parma and Rome, he took refuge with a farm family. They were around the dinner table when sixteen armed hoodlums stormed the house and ate the dinner. The gang's curiosity about Faber gave him an opening. By the end of the evening, the criminals had asked him to hear their confessions.

In 1540 the Pope had a new mission for Faber, as an advisor during conferences between Catholics and Protestants in Worms and then in Ratisbon (today's Regensburg), Germany. Faber realized that "the principal cause [of rebellion against the Church] was the perverse behavior of the clergy;

the following and imitation of Christ were the indispensable means of healing." Personal conversion was the solution, and the Spiritual Exercises were a powerful tool. For the first time, his person-to-person ministry dealt with educated and influential people. He directed church and government leaders in the Exercises.

While Faber was in Spain briefly, the princesses Doña Maria and Doña Juana and their guardian Doña Leonor developed a great affection for him. (Doña Leonor was so supportive that she was later dubbed "the mother of the Society.") When the Pope assigned him to Germany, they deputed their chaplains to accompany him. Walking and talking with Faber, both chaplains decided to become Jesuits.

Faber's influence with the bishops of Speyer and Mainz roused opposition among priests who had no interest in being reformed. However, when they came to know him personally, wayward clergy shifted from anger to esteem. By now, Faber had a reputation that led to a tug-of-war between Germany and Portugal for his services.

In obedience to Ignatius he went to Lisbon to make the Society known, then to Spain. In Gandía to lay the foundation stone of a new college founded by Duke Francis Borgia, the Jesuit spent a day in earnest conversation with the duke; the newly widowed Borgia was pondering a possible vocation to the Society.

The Pope's next assignment for Faber was to the Council of Trent. He went by way of Rome to see Ignatius again, after seven years apart. An oppressive heat wave covered the city that July. Only forty, Faber was worn out; he had been giving himself without counting the cost. His strength was spent. On July 31, 1546, he made a final Confession. The next afternoon, with Ignatius and all the Jesuits in the house around his bed, "he gave his soul to his Creator and Lord."

In 1872, he was beatified as Blessed Peter Faber; his feast is celebrated each August 2.

Francis Xavier (1506-1552)

Francis Xavier came of age as Portuguese navigators were encountering Asian "pagans," in their terminology. Monarchs and merchants saw potential profits from exotic produce—dyes, cloves, pepper. Missionaries saw countless human beings who knew nothing of Christ's saving message.

Kings controlled the trade through conquest; captains and bureaucrats made their profits through corruption. According to Xavier, "All go by the same road of 'I plunder, thou plunderest....'" He observed, "Some people suffer no remorse of conscience because they haven't got a conscience."

The Portuguese and Spanish carried Catholicism, often with the sword. Xavier imagined whole peoples brought to faith by the word.

Francis Xavier knew nothing of horizons. There was no limit to his voyaging in the name of Christ. He would go anywhere, endure any hardships, driven by an intense desire to bring people to Christ and to heaven.

Francis did not start out as a selfless adventurer. The youngest in a family of Navarre's minor nobility, he had his eye on a lucrative clerical position. For that goal, he studied philosophy and theology at the University of Paris and began to teach.

This castle in Navarre was home to the Xavier family. (Photo by Don Doll, S.J., courtesy of the Institute of Jesuit Sources)

On March 14, 1540, Ignatius sends Francis Xavier and Simão Rodrigues on a mission to India. (Engraving from Life of Ignatius *published by Barbé, 1609*)

Despite being forever short on money, he enjoyed the extracurricular side of student life. He was a good athlete and excelled at the high jump. With fellow students he sneaked out for late-night escapades until the sight of their ulcers from venereal disease scared him into chastity.

Francis and his roommate Peter Faber took in a third lodger in 1529, an older student named Ignatius Loyola, a Basque like Francis. However, their families had been on opposite sides in war, and Francis kept his defenses up, even when Ignatius offered financial assistance. While other students sought spiritual guidance from Ignatius, Francis resisted. Many years later, Ignatius called him "the lumpiest dough he had ever kneaded." By 1533, though, Ignatius had won Francis for God. The three roommates shared a sense of vocation and mission. Francis made the Spiritual Exercises during summer break of 1534.

Their studies completed, the first companions gathered in Venice, where Francis Xavier was ordained a priest in 1537. Celebrating Mass carried him into raptures; the altar server had to rouse him by tugging on his vestment. Blazing with love of God, his preaching went straight to people's hearts. He put love into action by working in a hospital while the companions tried to get to Jerusalem.

Instead, the Society of Jesus took shape in Rome. Before it was even solidified, the pious King John III of Portugal sought Jesuits to instruct Christian converts in India. Ignatius chose Rodrigues and Bobadilla, who fell ill. Ignatius explained the situation to Xavier. "Well then, here I am," Xavier responded. The next day, March 15, 1540, he set out for Asia and never looked back. Rodrigues having been reassigned to Portugal, Xavier launched out alone upon a voyage that would end only with his death.

In Goa on India's west coast, Xavier lodged in a hospital, tending to its most desperate cases. He visited prisons and preached in the church. Through the streets he walked, ringing a little bell, and children and slaves fell into a parade behind him. He composed religion lessons for them in sing-song rhymes. It was a far cry from philosophy classes in Paris! Yet Xavier also initiated the first Jesuit college in the world by accepting responsibility for Goa's new College of St. Paul and asking Ignatius for teachers.

Xavier made friends with the tough Portuguese soldiers, officials and merchants. He enjoyed people, was quick to praise others and sought to win their hearts for God.

Francis Xavier baptizes a youngster. (Sculpture in the college church, Vienna, photo by Thomas Lucas, S.J.)

Francis Xavier. (Statue by Louis Laumen, at Xavier College, Melbourne, Australia, photo courtesy of the Province of Australia)

News of souls in need drew him to the Paravas at the subcontinent's southernmost tip. These pearl-divers had been baptized *en masse*, practically uninstructed. With Tamil translators, Xavier went from village to village, baptizing babies, visiting the sick and grieving, teaching catechism, administering the sacraments and preaching. In each village he left a catechist in charge of nurturing the people's faith. Several times he barely escaped bullets and flames, as the hut he slept in was set ablaze by opponents of the Portuguese.

On the island of Mannar, he sometimes used a tree as a pulpit. Hearing that Xavier had baptized thousands, the rajah of Jaffna sent troops to stamp out Christianity by massacre and dispersed the surviving converts.

The eastern horizon opened up with word that two newly converted kings were seeking an evangelist for their people. Xavier's missionary soul caught fire—to bring whole peoples to Christ and to heaven! But should he leave India? He made a month-long retreat at the tomb of St. Thomas the Apostle (near today's Madras), seeking God's guidance. Convinced "that it is his will that I go to those regions," he set sail.

In the Moluccas (the Spice Islands), he reached the farthest Portuguese outpost, Banda (in today's Indonesia), Amboina, and the dangerously volcanic Ternate. His rhymed versions of the Creed and other prayers became popular songs. He ventured to "the perilous islands of Moro," where Christians had suffered intense persecution, and where poisoning and cannibalism were said to be routine. In remote villages, often at war, he rejoiced to find people eager for God, and he experienced "the abundant spiritual consolations that are to be found on these islands.... Islands of Hope in God...."

Like a scout, Xavier spent only a few months in each place, strengthening the Christian communities and planning for a team of Jesuits to establish bases for long-term ministry. His leadership consisted of going out in front, risking the unknown and paving the way. He inspired loyal devotion that spurred others to follow. Of his first meeting with Xavier, Jesuit Cosmoe de Torres recounted, "There and then, I wanted to follow in his footsteps." A Japanese named Anjiro declared, "I would lay down my life a hundred times for the love I bear him."

As the Provincial, Xavier returned to India to fulfill his administrative responsibilities. On the way he met Anjiro, who sparked yet another missionary yearning in the restless Jesuit: to go to Japan. Surely the Japanese would be more welcoming than Indians, he thought! In India he had encountered Hinduism and Islam without understanding their spiritual principles and retained a strong prejudice against them.

Cochin, south of Goa, was the provincial headquarters. To Xavier's disappointment, there were no letters waiting for him there, no words from his father in Christ or his "dearest brothers" in Italy, to whom he wrote, "the image of each one of you is stamped on my heart and soul." When letters finally arrived, he read and reread them and cut out the beloved signatures, which he kept in a copper reliquary worn on a cord around his neck.

Many of his own letters reveal Xavier's missionary approach, for example, emphasis on caring for the sick and dying; focus on basic truths rather than controversy; advice not to denounce sinners from the pulpit, but to speak privately— "The better friends you are, the straighter you can talk"—and suggestions for gently helping penitents get through painful confessions. Whether in the College of St. Paul or in the rigors of far-flung outposts, "it is not the actual physical exertion that counts...but the hearty readiness and spirit of faith...."

At last he could turn toward Japan. Anjiro was eager to share in the mission, along with Father Torres, Brother Juan Fernández de Oviedo and two servants. They hired the junk of Avan "the Pirate," who dodged storms and (other) pirates.

On August 15, 1549, they were ashore at Kagoshima in southern Japan. Xavier admired Japanese courtesy, honesty, rationality and sense of honor. Attempting the language, he remained dependant on Anjiro as translator. He baptized a young samurai who, as Bernard, became the first Japanese Jesuit. His convert Mary became the pillar of the local Christian community and a life-long devotée of Xavier.

Faced with hostility, Xavier set out for Kyoto, hoping to win the emperor's permission to evangelize the whole country. On their winter journey, Xavier, Fernández and Bernard were pelted with stones and shivered in squalid inns. One stretch saw them carrying the luggage of a nobleman's entourage. Running barefoot, Xavier was in high spirits, juggling an apple and sporting a Siamese cap.

"Mary of the Snows" blends European and Japanese styles. (Courtesy of the 26 Martyrs Shrine, Nagasaki, Japan)

Disappointment awaited them. The emperor would not give audience to an empty-handed nobody. Next they approached the ruler in Yamaguchi. This time they dressed in silk kimonos and bore intriguing European gifts—a clock, a music box, eyeglasses—and official parchments. Xavier declined any gifts from the ruler except permission to preach Christianity. Permission granted!

Four months of preaching, debates and conversions ensued. In September 1551, a plea came from a Portuguese acquaintance imprisoned in a Chinese dungeon. His captors expected an ambassador to come to China to negotiate his release. Xavier was excited, sensing an opening for the faith in China.

Yet there was no news from his Province. He must go back to India to investigate the state of affairs. *En route*, a package of letters—two-and-a-half years' worth—reached him. In one, Ignatius appointed him Provincial of the entire East. Back in Cochin, he dealt with problems that had accumulated during his absence, acting firmly and tenderly. A stern letter to Father Alfonso Cyprian ends, "O Cyprian, if you only guessed the love with which I write.... Francisco."

Meanwhile, he had one eye on China. Though he was forty-six and some gray peppered his black hair, his zeal was as dynamic as ever. He wrote to Ignatius about his plan to go to Canton with a Portuguese ambassador in 1552. From the many volunteers, Xavier chose Father Balthasar Gago (later redirected to Japan) and Brother Alvaro Ferreira, along with António China as an interpreter and Christôvão, an Indian servant.

In Malacca the plan fell apart. When the missionaries arrived in September on the island of Shangchuan ("Sancian," six miles off China's shore), they had no official standing; António had forgotten his native language; Ferreira soon departed, fearing imprisonment and death. With the approach of winter, Portuguese merchants and smugglers left the island, after burning their straw beach huts.

A Chinese merchant who had agreed to spirit Xavier, António and Christôvão ashore did not show up. Daily, hourly, Xavier scanned the coastline. "The danger of all dangers," he wrote, "would be to lose trust and confidence." Cold and hunger penetrated his bones.

Jesus Christ set Francis Xavier's heart afire with missionary zeal. This Japanese portrait was created in Brother Giovanni Niccolo's art academy in Japan, founded in 1583 to teach the faith and to inspire through images. The words, "It is enough, Lord, it is enough," are from the prayer "Suscipe" in the Spiritual Exercises.

On November 21, he fell ill with a high fever. Despite António's care, death was near. In delirium, the Jesuit spoke of his brothers in the Society and talked ardently with God in several languages, including his Basque mother tongue, then slipped into a coma. On December 1 he regained consciousness. He invoked the Trinity and Mary and repeatedly cried out, "Jesus, Son of David, have mercy on me!" António later reported that, a little before dawn on December 3, "I put a candle in his hand. Then, with the name of Jesus on his lips, he rendered his soul...with great calm."

Francis Xavier's body was taken to Malacca, then to Goa, much honored and lamented. For years many witnesses attested to its preservation. He was canonized in 1622. December 3 is the feast day of this patron saint of missions.

Ignatius blesses his spiritual sons and sends them on mission into the world.
(Engraving from Life of Ignatius *published by Barbé, 1609)*

Chapter II

HEROES OF FAITH

*"I have made a free oblation of myself to your Divine Majesty,
both of life and of death, and I hope that you will give me grace and force to perform.
This is all I desire. Amen." (Edmund Campion, S.J.)*

Aloysius Gonzaga

Stanislaus Kostka

Edmund Campion

Heroes of Faith
The 16ᵗʰ Century

The second generation of Jesuits consisted of men born into the new world that had opened up at the beginning of the sixteenth century. Their youthful dreams must have carried them across the seas with Portuguese and Spanish galleons to the unexplored Americas or to Asia's fabled ancient cities. They may have imagined heroic exploits. In some countries, persecution drove Catholics underground.

Across Europe, Catholics and Protestants faced off in pulpits and classrooms. Words were not the only weapons involved; the conflict drew blood on Europe's battlefields.

The men of this age expected challenges. They exerted their strength to the utmost under God's banner, with courage and fidelity. These Jesuits were adventurers. They were heroes. What made them saints was the purpose that drove them: to honor God and to lead their fellow human beings to heaven. They had powerful models in Francis Xavier and Peter Faber.

Underlying their dedication was the choice each man had made in the Spiritual Exercises: to live and die under the standard of Christ. This radical commitment was the legacy of their spiritual father, Ignatius Loyola.

■ *The Spiritual Exercises take the retreatant with Jesus to Jerusalem (left) and to the moment of choice (right) before his Cross. (Mural by José M. Fernandes Machado, S.J. in the Ignacio de Azeveda Novitiate Chapel, São Paulo, Brazil. Photo courtesy of Rodrigo Zaniolo)*

■ *Page 27: Aloysius & Campion courtesy of Jesuit Sources, Stanislaus courtesy of the Province of Belgium*

The Exploding Sixteenth Century

The ferment of the early sixteenth century became an explosion, or a series of explosions, by the century's second half. The Society of Jesus was itself one of those explosions. By 1580, 5000 men had joined the Society. The only way to explain such growth is the convergence of a powerful spiritual gift with the deep spiritual need of an age. It was a time of greatness.

All over the world, men caught the spark.

At the Society's Roman College, the finest professors taught an international student body of top caliber. No motives of wealth or worldly advancement would figure in a Jesuit vocation, no positions of prominence in the Church. For the greater glory of God and to help souls, Jesuits went to the center of all that was afoot in the world.

Church reform had moved beyond religious protest. Battle lines were drawn. England's queens followed the ruthless example of their father, Henry VIII. Mary Tudor killed Protestants; Elizabeth I killed Catholics. During Elizabeth's long reign, brave Catholic laity and priests lived dangerously.

On the European continent, princes entrenched themselves in religious warfare, and religious leaders took to the pulpits in what they saw as a great battle for the soul of Christendom.

The Council of Trent (three sessions between 1545 and 1563) had drafted the Catholic Church's plan for internal reform. Clerical training and religious education figured prominently. The need for religious educators and books and for spiritual leadership was obvious. The Jesuits' thorough academic preparation equipped them in these fields. Their commitment to meet needs identified by the Pope made them available. The Society of Jesus became integral to the Church's renewal.

Ignatius considered university teaching crucial to the religious struggle. Jesuit colleges (roughly comparable to today's senior high schools) addressed both personal development and the needs of the times through theology, spirituality and high-quality instruction in all fields. They equipped men well for priesthood or for committed lay life.

Through preaching, Jesuits reached out to the general population, appealing to the spirit through the mind and heart.

On the world scene, Europe had shifted rapidly from relative isolation to exploration to colonial domination. The Spanish and Portuguese were starting to build empires in the Americas. Older religious orders accompanied them first, zealous Franciscans, Dominicans and Augustinians. Before the new Society of Jesus even had its feet on the ground, its men were in the missions. All the orders walked a fine line when dealing with governments. Only the rulers could open for them the doors to mission lands. Yet conquistadors and colonists often violated the indigenous peoples whom the missionaries were evangelizing.

It was an era of absolutes. One was the belief that only through Catholic faith could anyone reach heaven. Missionaries labored to bring salvation to people who had never heard of Christ or the Church. They mirrored the divine love for humanity that showed itself in Jesus. Like him, they emptied themselves for the sake of others—to help souls.

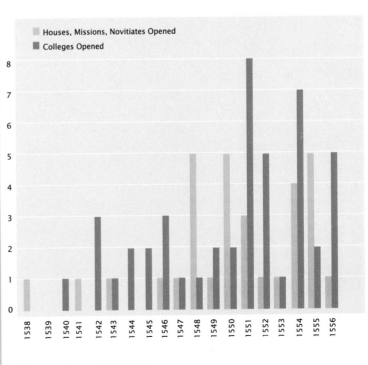

■ *Annual growth 1538-1556*
(Courtesy of Thomas Lucas, S.J., from Landmarking*)*

Peter Canisius (1521-1597)

Peter Canisius was a leading figure of the Catholic response to the Protestant Reformation in Germany, a hotbed of religious controversy.

Theology was not the only factor in Germany's shift toward Protestantism. Mercenaries of the Catholic Emperor Charles V were antagonizing the common people. Many priests and bishops were materialistic and self-indulgent. Most Catholics were uninstructed. The Council of Trent brought Church leaders together to consider the problems and plan a Counter-Reformation within the Church. Education in the faith and spiritual renewal were among the top priorities.

A college student at Germany's illustrious Cologne University was wrestling with his future. His father, Meister Jakop Kanis, was a prosperous businessman and civic leader in Nijmegen, the Netherlands. Drawn to serve God, Peter could not imagine following in his father's footsteps. He studied theology, but with no clear purpose.

A childhood memory kept coming back to him. An old lady had told the small Peter that a new religious order was about to begin and that he would belong to it. Now twenty-one, he met Alvaro Alfonso, a Jesuit novice, who told him about the Society of Jesus, not yet two years old. Was this to be his future? Alfonso told him that one of the Society's founders, Father Peter Faber, was in Mainz. Peter Kanis went there to learn more.

The young man's sincerity impressed Faber, who agreed to direct him in the Spiritual Exercises. On May 8, 1543, his twenty-second birthday, he entered the Society. The old lady had seen clearly.

Peter finished his theology studies, published several books and taught Scripture in the

University of Cologne until his ordination in June, 1546. Cardinal Otto von Truchsess took this young scholar to the Council of Trent as his theological advisor in 1547. After the Council's first session, Ignatius called Kanis—now known by the Latinzied name "Canisius"—to Rome.

Canisius volunteered enthusiastically for the new Jesuit college in Messina as "cook or gardener or porter or student or professor." Not surprisingly, his assignment was to teach. His heart turned back to Germany, though, with a brooding concern. In 1549 Pope Paul III himself asked Canisius to defend the Church in Germany from the attacks of Protestant theologians. From that moment, "I would long... to spend myself utterly in life and death for [Germany's] salvation."

Still in his twenties, Canisius felt the weight of his mission. Before leaving Rome, he prayed before the tomb of St. Peter, his patron saint, and felt "great consolation" and confidence in the support of the Apostles. He experienced the heart of Jesus opening to him. "I seemed to see within it," he wrote later, "and Thou didst invite me and bid me to drink the waters of salvation from that fountain."

Assigned to the University of Ingolstadt, Canisius sought to win minds and hearts. "Dear God, what a task it is to keep the Catholics in the ancient Faith!" Students appreciated his lectures and personal attention, but hopes for a Jesuit college there evaporated. He moved in 1552 to the new Jesuit college in Vienna, Austria. He also did pastoral work among the sick, the poor, prisoners and military veterans. He preached tirelessly in Vienna's cathedral. His words stirred his listeners so deeply that they protested when he was absent.

Venite filij, audite me : timorem Domini docebo vos. Pſal. 33.

Venite, aſcendamus ad montem Domini, & ad domum Dei Iacob, & docebit nos vias ſuas, & ambulabimus in ſemitis eius. Eſai.2.Mich.4.

■ *"Christ and the Children" appears in* Small Catechism *by Peter Canisius, published in Cologne in 1563—first published in 1555. (Reproduced in Bernhard Duhr's* Geschichte der Jesuiten in den Laendern deutscher Zunge, *Vol. I. Freiburg: 1907, p. 79.)*

Austria's Catholic King Ferdinand wanted a manual to prepare priests for educating parishioners. The responsibility to write it fell upon Canisius. His *Summary of Christian Doctrine* for college students appeared in 1555. In question-and-answer format, it concentrated heavily on issues debated by Protestants. In quick succession followed a children's version, then one for secondary students. These catechisms made the name "Canisius" synonymous with "catechism" in German. They went through 200 editions in many languages within his lifetime and remained in use until the nineteenth century. Canisius was the first Jesuit to publish a book.

Friendship led King Ferdinand to confide to Canisius "his most intimate secrets, depositing in my breast the hidden things of his heart." Warmth and mutual appreciation marked his relationships.

■ *Christopher Clavius (1538-1612), a German, was called the "most influential teacher of the Renaissance" and "the Euclid of the sixteenth century." He taught mathematics at the Roman College for forty-five years. His influence circled the world through his Jesuit pupils as well as through the Gregorian calendar, which he developed.*

Jesuit Education and the *Ratio Studiorum*

Ignatius agreed in 1547 to establish a college in Messina, Sicily. By the time he died, there were fifty-one colleges. First envisioned as preparing new Jesuits, they quickly opened to lay men and diocesan priests. The Society was transforming its primary mission from itinerant preaching to stable institutions with sustained impact.

Jesuit colleges (secondary schools) and universities constituted the first worldwide educational system. For cohesiveness and quality control, Father General Acquaviva published in 1599 a "Plan of Studies" based upon consultation and carefully refined.

The plan *(ratio)* describes staff roles and outlines curriculum: integrating Scholastic theology and philosophy (including scientific subjects covered in "natural philosophy") with new fields of Renaissance humanism. Jesuits were soon writing textbooks. Ignatius had provided for a good press at the Roman College.

"Jesuit education" came to be synonymous with spiritual commitment and intellectual excellence.

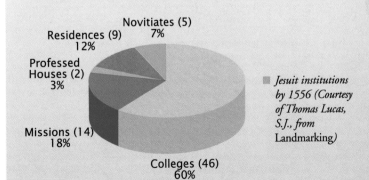

Novitiates (5) 7%
Residences (9) 12%
Professed Houses (2) 3%
Missions (14) 18%
Colleges (46) 60%

■ *Jesuit institutions by 1556 (Courtesy of Thomas Lucas, S.J., from* Landmarking*)*

Like this anonymous Jesuit, Canisius was a tireless and highly popular preacher. This woodcut is in Schere Georg's Catechismus oder Kinderlehr, *published in Bruck in 1600. (Reproduced in Bernhard Duhr's* Geschichte der Jesuiten in den Laendern deutscher Zunge, *Vol. I. Freiburg: 1907, pp. 455, 456)*

Appointed provincial superior for the new Province of Upper Germany, Canisius founded college after college, eighteen in all. He must have applied his father's business sense after all—raising funds, acquiring land, negotiating contracts and supervising construction for eighteen institutions.

Civic and religious leaders vied for Canisius's presence at conferences, such as the inter-religious assembly at Worms (1557), where he debated the Protestant theological champion, Melanchthon.

The Jesuit's effectiveness angered his adversaries. Some made a joke of his name, connecting "Canisius" with the Latin word *canis,* "dog."

He founded his last university in Fribourg, Switzerland, in 1582, but only after the skeptical Swiss authorities were won over by getting to know him. There he served as the first president of a Jesuit university.

In retirement he continued writing, mainly spiritual works. Even when the provincial superior blocked his work, Canisius communicated only praise of the man to Father General Borgia. The great controversialist had a sweetness of spirit that did not desert him in illness and old age. As long as possible he continued the preaching that drew so many to God.

The college student who had been uncertain about his life had become a man of purpose and achievement—for the greater glory of God. The young priest who had prayed to the Apostles had become the "Second Apostle of Germany." His decisive impact had turned the religious tide for the Church among the German people.

The results of a stroke and illnesses afflicted Canisius from 1591 until his death on December 21, 1597. His last words were "Blessed God, God, God."

In canonizing Peter Canisius in 1925, Pope Pius XI added the title "Doctor (teacher) of the Church." In classroom or pulpit, in writing or debating—he was a teacher of faith. His feast day is April 27.

Edmund Campion (1540-1581)

King Henry VIII required all citizens to acknowledge the monarch as head of the Church in England. Catholics loyal to the universal Church lost property, position and even their lives. They practiced their religion in secret and were starved for the sacraments. Priests risked death. A Catholic seminary in Douai, France, trained priests who would re-enter the country to minister in secret, suspected of treason.

The Society of Jesus opened a mission to England in 1580, "to preach the Gospel, to minister the Sacraments, to instruct the simple, to reform sinners, to confute errors," in Edmund Campion's words. Everyone knew that the English Mission would be a field of martyrs.

If ever a rising star shot across the sky, it was Edmund Campion. Talent, honors, a successful career....

And prison, torture, heaven....

■ *Jesuits on the English Mission were always in danger of arrest. (Courtesy of the Institute of Jesuit Sources)*

■ *Edmund Campion*
(Courtesy of the Institute of Jesuit Sources)

Words were his instruments. At thirteen, Edmund was chosen to deliver his school's address welcoming the new Queen Mary Tudor. By twenty-four he was such a popular lecturer at St. John's College, Oxford, that his followers called themselves "Campionites" and imitated him. Again he was chosen to welcome a queen, this time Elizabeth I, in 1564. Well educated herself, she was impressed with his Latin oration. They would meet again.

Though baptized a Catholic, he had been brought up an Anglican and was ordained a deacon in the Church of England. However, reading the Church Fathers led him to believe that Roman Catholicism was the authentic heir of the apostolic church.

He had decided. He had to act.

Campion went to Douai, France, to study for the priesthood. In 1573, degree in hand, he walked to Rome, as had Ignatius, to become a

Jesuit: "Hereby I have taken upon me a special kind of warfare under the banner of obedience, and eke resigned all my interest or possibilitie of wealth, honour, pleasure, and other worldlie felicitie." Assigned to the Austrian province, he taught, becoming the foremost orator in Prague. He wrote and directed plays for his students.

The curtain was about to rise on his own drama as an underground priest. He was in the first wave of the Society's new English Mission, "for the glorie of God and benefit of souls."

Elizabeth's spies were alert. At his Dover landing on June 24, 1580, they snared a "Mr. Edmonds" but could not prove their suspicions. He made it to London, continually dodging "so many eyes, so many tongues, so many scouts" and changing his name and clothing constantly.

In hiding, he wrote a manifesto, later called "Campion's Brag," declaring the religious purpose of the Jesuit mission and professing loyalty to "the Queen, my Sovereign Lady" in all temporal matters. Campion describes the Jesuits' commitment "cheerfully to carry the cross you shall lay upon us, and never to despair your recovery, while we have a man left to enjoy your Tyburn, or to be racked with your torments, or consumed with your prisons." Prophetic words!

Ministry to faithful—but hidden—Catholics took him from one private home to another for the next year, always in disguise, always a step ahead of pursuers, seldom more than one night in one place. Priest-hunters were on his trail. Their moment came. Their man was George Eliot (not the novelist).

On Sunday, July 16, 1581, Eliot wormed his way into Lyford Grange, Berkshire, for Mass. Realizing that the visiting priest was the "seditious Jesuit," he informed the local magistrate. A search party could find nothing. Campion and two other priests were in "priest holes" cleverly concealed within the walls. Finally, a glimmer of light revealed the hiding place. It was the beginning of the end.

Campion found himself in the Tower of London's "little ease," a cell so small that a man could neither stand nor lie down. Soon the Queen herself received Campion and tried to lure him with the promise of a successful career in the Church of England. His only fault, she said, was being a Catholic priest—"my greatest glory," he responded.

Torture was the next step, but in four sessions of being stretched on the rack he would utter no treason, nor would he accuse his friends, who suffered similar tortures.

Anthony Criminali (1520-1549) First Jesuit Martyr

The first Jesuit to die a martyr's death was Anthony Criminali. Faber directed him in the Spiritual Exercises, Loyola admitted him to the Society, and Xavier assigned him to Cape Cormorin, on India's southern tip, in 1543. Xavier described him as "a holy man...beloved by native Christians, pagans, and Moslems."

Angered by their conquerors' greed, Indian warriors attacked the Portuguese settlement and all connected with it. The missionary stayed with his defenseless flock of native Christians. Bleeding from a lance wound, Criminali staggered toward the chapel to die. Struck again, he again rose. A third blow felled him, and a warrior severed his head.

The Church honors him with the title Servant of God.

■ *Engraving from Matthias Tanner's book of Jesuit martyrs [1675] (photo courtesy of Thomas Lucas, S.J.)*

On November 20, Campion and seven others were tried. He could not raise his injured hand for the courtroom oath. A fellow defendant assisted him and noticed that his fingernails were missing. Campion professed, "If our religion make us traitors, we are worthy to be condemned; but otherwise are...as good subjects as ever the Queen had." Eliot gave perjured testimony that Campion had conspired against the Queen's life and supported a foreign invasion.

The verdict: guilty of treason.

The sentence: to be hanged, drawn, and quartered.

SOCIETAS EUROPÆA.

P. Edmundus Campianus, et P. Alexander Briantus, Angli S. I. pro Fide suspensi et secti Londini in Anglia A. 1581. 1. Decembris.

C. S. d.   M.K. f.

■ *Edmund Campion and Alexander Briant were hanged, then drawn and quartered. (Engraving from Matthias Tanner's book of Jesuit martyrs [1675], photo courtesy of Thomas Lucas, S.J.)*

The execution: December 1, rain and mud. Campion, Alexander Briant, S.J., and Ralph Sherwin (a diocesan priest) emerged from the Tower. "God save you all, gentlemen," Campion greeted the onlookers. The three condemned men were tied to hurdles and dragged by horses to Tyburn, the place of execution.

A cart stood under the gallows. Campion climbed it and, with the noose around his neck, professed, "I am a Catholic man and a priest; in that faith have I lived and in that faith I intend to die. If you esteem my religion treason, then I am guilty; as for other treason, I never committed any. God is my judge." He forgave the jury and prayed for the Queen.

Then the cart was pulled away. When he was cut down, the rest of the sentence was carried out: his heart and intestines drawn out, his body hacked into quarters. His spirit had already mounted victoriously above treachery and lies.

"I have no more to say," his manifesto declared, "but to recommend your case and mine to Almightie God, the Searcher of Hearts, who send us His grace, and set us at accord before the day of payment, to the end we may at last be friends in heaven, when all injuries shall be forgotten." His name and words still ring out with courage and truth.

Edmund Campion was canonized in 1970. He is celebrated on December 1 each year, with other Jesuit martyrs of England and Wales.

Robert Southwell (1561-1595)

■ *(Permission of the Society of Jesus Office of Press and Information)*

"Never safe for even the briefest moment," the poet Robert Southwell served on the English Mission from 1586 till his capture in 1591. He wrote (and Henry Garnet, S.J., printed) the only religious literature available to English Catholics.

Remaining gracious during terrible tortures and a long, harsh imprisonment, Southwell betrayed no companions. On February 21, 1595, he was hanged, drawn and quartered.

Southwell was canonized in 1970 and is remembered with the other English martyrs on December 1.

A Child My Choice

Let folly praise that fancy loves, I praise and love that child,
Whose heart no thought, whose tongue no word,
    whose hand no deed defiled.
I praise him most, I love him best, all praise and love is his;
While him I love, in him I live, and cannot live amiss.

Love's sweetest mark, laud's highest theme,
    man's most desired light,
To love him life, to leave him death, to live in him delight.
He mine by gift, I his by debt, thus each to other due.
First friend he was, best friend he is,
    all times will try him true...

José de Anchieta (1534-1597)

Jesuits entered Brazil's vast mission fields and dangerous flashpoints with zeal and courage. Traditional local animosities and European rivalries intensified the dangers. When indigenous Tamoyos clashed with their Portuguese conquerors, French Protestant colonizers supplied arms to the Tamoyos. Father Manuel de Nóbrega took the bold initiative of venturing into hostile territory to negotiate a treaty with the Tamoyos in 1563.

Nóbrega and José de Anchieta founded the missions that became São Paulo and Rio de Janiero, writing the first pages of a new civilization.

As the Society's mission matured into a province, volunteers swelled Jesuit numbers to 150 by 1584, while Anchieta was provincial superior.

At nineteen, José de Anchieta would not let a painful spinal condition dampen his eagerness to carry the Gospel to a "new world." He built upon his strengths: gentle courage, endurance and a gift for languages. The world remembers him as "Apostle of Brazil," co-founder of two great cities and "Father of Brazilian Literature."

■ *Theatrical performances were tools of Jesuit pedagogy which Anchieta carried with him from Europe to America. (Courtesy of the Institute of Jesuit Sources)*

Born in the Canary Islands in 1534, he went to the university at Coimbra, Portugal, at fifteen. He drank in its intellectual and religious enthusiasm and entered the Society in 1551. A fellow student affectionately dubbed him "the canary of Coimbra."

José asked to be sent to the Brazil mission. Six days after making simple vows in 1553, he sailed west, past the Canary Islands, never to return.

At the Jesuit mission of São Vincente, his first task was to learn the local language, Tupi-Guaraní. His gift for languages would now have an apostolic purpose.

Father Manuel de Nóbrega took José with him to help establish a new mission and school in the small village of Piratininga, which would become São Paulo. In "a poor little house that serves as school, infirmary, dormitory, dining hall, kitchen and food store," José was teaching Tupi and Portuguese children and Jesuit scholastics. Despite this chaotic environment, he managed to compose a Tupi grammar. He added a catechism, booklets for sacramental preparation and a dictionary in Tupi in his two decades at São Paulo.

José recognized and named the "injustices and wrongs" inflicted by the Portuguese on the people they had conquered. A mission of peace took him into the jaws of death. He accompanied Fr. Nóbrega as interpreter and spokesman on a peace mission to hostile Tamoyos. José's sense of justice made him an essential collaborator. His personal charm and his knowledge of the local language and customs contributed to the eventual peace. He won over a Tamoyo leader who had intended to murder the two Jesuits.

For three months, he was confined as a hostage. The Tamoyo chief assured him, "My son, José, have no fear; ...I shall not allow you to be killed, for I know you speak the truth."

In a gesture of respect, the Indians offered him their daughters and were astonished that he declined. José recognized his need for strength to be faithful to his vow of chastity. He found the grace he sought in Mary. He turned his prayers and praise into a long Latin poem in Mary's honor, which he memorized, then wrote out after his release.

His ordination in 1566 opened a decade of new responsibilities, first as superior at São Vicente. In addition to administrative duties,

Paul Miki (1564-1597)
John de Goto (1578-1597)
James Kisai (1533-1597)

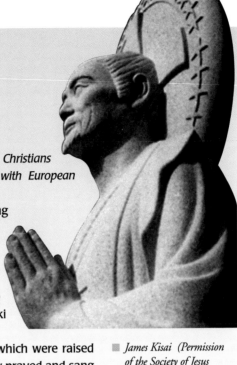

Forty-five years after Francis Xavier's departure, Japan's Christians numbered about 200,000. Under suspicion of sympathizing with European colonial ambitions, they faced execution.

Paul Miki was an accomplished preacher, approaching ordination. John de Goto was a catechist before entering the Society. Brother James Kisai, a catechist, had separated from his wife after her return to Buddhism.

All three were arrested in Osaka, along with Spanish Franciscans and lay leaders. After a forced winter march, the prisoners arrived in Nagasaki on February 5, 1597. Miki renewed his vows and the other Jesuits pronounced theirs.

That morning, twenty-six men embraced their crosses, which were raised on a hill above the city. With 4000 mourning Christians, they prayed and sang hymns. John de Goto spotted his father in the crowd, and they encouraged each other. Paul Miki preached his last sermon and forgave his executioner. As the soldiers pierced each martyr's breast with a lance, Miki cried out, "Into your hands, O Lord, I commend my spirit."

"Martyrs' Hill" became a shrine. Over 5000 Christians were martyred in the next half-century, including thirty-three Jesuits. Paul Miki and his companions were canonized in 1862 and are celebrated annually on February 6.

■ *James Kisai (Permission of the Society of Jesus Office of Press and Information)*

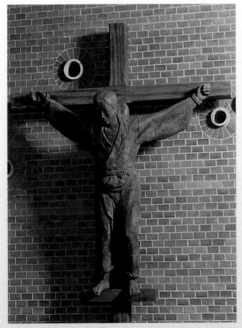

■ *Paul Miki (Courtesy of the 26 Martyrs Shrine, Nagasaki, Japan)*

■ *Brother Lawrence Ryosai (1525-1592) was the first to enter the Society in Japan, in 1556. (Bernard had gone to India and Europe in 1551.) Nearly blind, he had been a minstrel. Lawrence became a highly effective catechist. (Painting by Machida Gyokko, 26 Martyrs Shrine, Nagasaki, Japan. Photo courtesy of the Society of Jesus Office of Press and Information)*

■ *Brazilian students reenact a scene from the life of Anchieta, marking the fourth centennial of his death in 1997. It is a fitting tribute to one who taught through drama. (Yearbook S.J. 1999, courtesy of the Society of Jesus Office of Press and Information)*

Fr. Anchieta was out on the mission road. But there were no roads. He walked mountain ridges and navigated whitewater. His canoe once plummeted over a waterfall. He learned another language and began to evangelize the Maramomi people.

"Nothing is too arduous," he declared, "that has as its purpose the honor of God and the salvation of souls."

Anchieta wrote dramatizations of biblical and other religious stories for his students to perform, to bring his lessons alive. These plays in Latin, Portuguese and Tupi won him the title of "Father of Brazilian National Literature."

As provincial superior (1577), he governed with a gentleness unfamiliar to the rugged missionaries. Some considered him "too soft." Nonetheless, he was universally respected for his obvious goodness and insight.

Up and down Brazil, he traveled to Jesuit missions. Because his hunched spine made horseback-riding difficult, he usually traveled inland on foot. But along Brazil's 1500-mile Atlantic coastline, this son of the Canary Islands was at home in his small, swift sailboat, the *Santa Ursula*, piloted by Brother Francisco Dias.

Ill health led him to ask for another assignment in 1587. In the vast mission of Espiritu Santo, Anchieta was again a catechist. He traveled deep into the wilderness to carry the Good News of Jesus Christ to remote settings. He invited new Christians to gather in villages.

Through four decades he had spent himself for others. In 1592 it was time to retire. He asked the rector to send him on mission, one last time, "and Our Lord willed to make me assistant to Fr. Diogo Fernandes in this village of Reritiba [now renamed Anchieta] to help in the instruction of the Indians." Teaching the faith: it had always been his heart's desire.

Feeling death approach in 1597, he wrote his last poem, honoring Mary. On the morning of June 9, he asked to receive Holy Communion. Then his spirit took flight to God.

Pope John Paul II beatified Blessed José de Anchieta in 1980. The Church celebrates his memorial on June 9.

■ *José de Ancheita plied the coastal waters, visiting the Society's Brazilian Province. Many stories tell of his affection for animals and birds. (Yearbook S.J. 1999, courtesy of the Society of Jesus Office of Press and Information)*

Stanislaus Kostka (1550-1568)

Noble parents like Stanislaus Kostka's, who wanted their sons to "do well," definitely did not have the Jesuits in mind. The new Society hardly seemed respectable. A monk's life was stable, but a Jesuit would move from place to place as opportunities for ministry emerged. The Society owned no property, and Jesuits declined appointments to the hierarchy and the power and riches that went with them. Ambition would not motivate a Jesuit vocation— only a deeply felt call from God, often followed at great personal cost.

■ *Stanislaus Kostka (Courtesy of the Province of Belgium)*

Inner steel is not always visible. Stanislaus Kostka's older brother Paul mistook his quiet manner for weakness. How wrong he was! From a place of deep interior strength, Stanislaus could withstand the bully's abuse. He could choose his own path in life and walk it for nearly 1000 miles. He could cheerfully face an early death.

Even as a child on the family estate in Rostkow, Poland, Stanislaus responded whole-heartedly to God. "In the first prayer which I can remember," he later wrote, "I gave myself totally to God."

When Stanislaus was fourteen, his father Jan enrolled him and Paul in Vienna's Jesuit school, accompanied by three servants and Jan Bilinski, their tutor. Intoxicated with his new freedom, sixteen-year-old Paul turned to carefree self-indulgence. Stanislaus took his studies seriously and continued to develop his spiritual life.

■ *The Church of the Gesù replaced that of Santa Maria della Strada as the Society's spiritual center. Begun in Ignatius's last year, it was built under the patronage of Cardinal Alessandro Farnese and dedicated in 1584. Giacomo Della Porta designed this façade, which influenced Jesuit churches around the world. Giacomo da Vignola created an interior suited to the Society's apostolic and devotional goals, with good visibility for preaching, space for many confessionals, and side altars dedicated to the saints, especially martyrs. (Courtesy of the Society of Jesus Office of Press and Information)*

Francis Borgia (1510-1572)

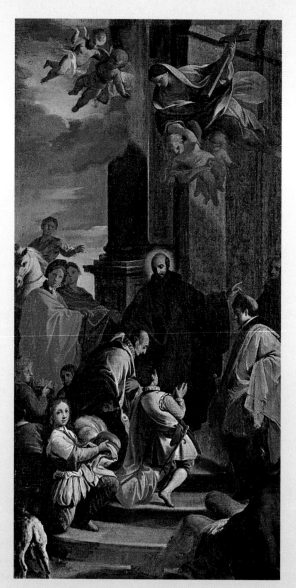

Francis Borgia, Duke of Gandía (Permission of the Society of Jesus Office of Press and Information)

Offspring of a scandalous ancestry, court page, Duke of Gandía, trusted friend of Emperor Charles V, husband, father of eight, founder of a college.... Francis Borgia wanted more. He wanted a life of prayer.

When his beloved wife died in 1546, Borgia's vocation to the Society blossomed. Ignatius told him to fulfill his responsibilities to his children first. Five years later he laid aside his titles and estates. His son served at his first Mass, celebrated in the Loyola castle chapel.

Borgia's interest in education prompted him to support the Roman College and found many Jesuit colleges as an administrator in Spain. He began the Society's Church of the Gesu in Rome. Though he was elected the third superior general, Pope and rulers continued to rely on him. After a taxing diplomatic mission, he died in 1572, having begged, "Fathers and Brothers, forgive me for the love of God."

Canonized in 1671, he is celebrated on October 3.

Francis Borgia, third Father General (Courtesy of Thomas Lucas, S.J.)

Ignatius receives Francis Borgia into the Society. The Duke's retinue accompanied him to Rome. (Painting by Andrea Pozzo, S.J., Church of St. Ignatius, Rome. Photo courtesy of Thomas Lucas, S.J.)

The brothers quarreled over everything. Stanislaus wanted modest lodgings in a quiet setting. Paul insisted on comfortable rooms in a mansion that would accommodate two cousins as well as their own entourage. Maybe Paul was feeling defensive about his behavior; he took it out on Stanislaus, with insults and abuse. When Stanislaus knelt in prayer late at night, the cousins pretended to be sleep-walking and trampled on him.

Months of mistreatment actually strengthened Stanislaus's inner core. If anything, his commitment deepened. However, his health suffered. Anticipating death, he asked to receive Holy Communion, but their Lutheran landlord would not allow a priest in the house. Bilinski was in the sickroom when Stanislaus told him that St. Barbara (the patron saint of his sodality) was coming from heaven with two angels, "and one of them brings me the Body of my Lord Jesus Christ."

More ineffective medical treatment followed. Then Stanislaus saw Mary, who placed the child Jesus in his arms and told him, "I want you to join the Society of Jesus." The next morning he was well, to the amazement of his doctors.

Stanislaus was eager to follow the calling so powerfully revealed to him. The road ahead would require all his persistence and will power. Paul resumed his bullying words and blows. His ultimate insult was "you Jesuit!"

Knowing that his father would object, Stanislaus was developing a plan. He would apply to Peter Canisius, Provincial of the Society's German Province. Very early on Sunday, August 10, 1567, he set out in disguise for Augsburg.

In fifteen days he walked the 450 miles (725 kilometers), only to be told, "Father Canisius isn't here. He's in Dillingen." It was another day's walk. Stanislaus would not stop to rest. On to Dillingen!

Canisius saw the sincerity and depth of this seventeen-year-old. The young noble did domestic chores; he was humble and adaptable. They agreed that Rome would be farther from his father's reach. Stanislaus walked on to Munich and from there set out for Rome. With two Jesuits, the determined candidate spent another month on the road. They crossed the Alps and arrived in Rome on October 25. Since August 10 Stanislaus had walked more than 930 miles (1500 kilometers),

following God's call. Father General Francis Borgia received him as a novice.

In a letter of recommendation Canisius wrote, "an excellent, intelligent young man" who "wished to advance as much as he could in the path of holiness.... We expect great things of him." The novice-master, Giulio Fazio, would later describe Stanislaus as humble, obedient, joyful and prayerful. The novice devoted himself to his tasks in the kitchen.

Jan Kostka reacted violently to the news that his son had joined the Society of Jesus. "If you persist in this folly, do not try to set foot in Poland again...instead of the golden chains I was keeping ready for you, you will find iron chains and a dungeon."

Stanislaus replied, "I do hope that in time you will give me back your former affection."

A premonition told Stanislaus that he would be in heaven for the feast of Mary's Assumption, August 15, 1568. On August 10 he fell sick, apparently with the malarial fever that was rampant in Rome. On the afternoon of the 14th, the patient's condition worsened. He was anointed and received Holy Communion. As his body weakened, his spirits rose. His fellow novices visited in the infirmary, and he chatted cheerfully with them.

When they had gone to bed, he prayed joyfully, "My heart is ready, O God, my heart is ready!" He begged to be placed on the floor to die, and a mattress was set there for him. On August 15, at 3 a.m., he seemed to see Mary, with saints and angels, coming to take him to heaven. He was eighteen years old.

Paul Kostka later became a Jesuit brother. In 1605, Stanislaus Kostka became the first Jesuit to be beatified. He was canonized in 1726. November 13 is his feast day.

Aloysius Gonzaga (1568-1591)

The Gonzaga clan figured among northern Italy's most powerful rulers. Aloysius Gonzaga's parents, the Marquis and Marchioness of Castiglione, moved in Spain's royal circle. Don Ferrante was a victorious commander and a Prince of the Holy Roman Empire. A cousin was a prominent cardinal. Gonzaga ambitions involved ruthless plots, poisonings and assassinations.

Starkly contrasting choices lay before young Aloysius Gonzaga. The massive stone palace where he was born in 1568 was a center of privilege and intrigue. Lust for power was a fundamental principle. His father taught him the arts of war. His mother fostered different aspirations, religious ones.

In the military camp where Don Ferrante took his firstborn, the five-year-old Aloysius almost killed himself when a gun he was playing with fired. He also picked up some vocabulary that shocked his mother. However, prayer, study and compassion for the poor eventually replaced his warrior interests. The proud father expected his heir to be a wise ruler.

Studies in the Medici court in Florence and an appointment in Madrid as a court page surrounded Aloysius with comfort and power. The teenager felt that his soul was under assault. Courageously he combated temptation through intense penitential practices. The Gonzagas were luxurious and self-indulgent; he wore shabby clothing and controlled his impulses. The Gonzagas were imperious; he obeyed.

Aloysius matured spiritually through his reading, the guidance of Jesuit confessors, the sacraments and prayer. At fifteen he decided to enter the Society of Jesus. Furious, his father would not hear of it. He would not give up his heir, surely not to an order with no prospects of power or wealth! Aloysius would not give up his vocation.

Father and son were well-matched. Three years of warfare followed. The Marquis set troops in motion—the parish priest, a cousin who was a religious superior, a bishop, a spiritual advisor—but all attested that the young man's vocation seemed authentic. Aloysius was sent on a tour of splendid Italian courts with his brother Rodolfo. He refused his elaborate new wardrobe and traveled in a black tunic. The strongest assault was his father's tears. Despite their conflicts, they loved each other.

Aloysius resisted every siege. Finally Don Ferrante capitulated, and his heir formally abdicated his inheritance to Rodolfo on November 2, 1585. "His delight in coming to the succession," Aloysius said, "cannot be as great as mine in renouncing it."

The next day he was on the road to the novitiate in Rome. There he would be occupied with domestic chores and studies, and the novice master would have to moderate his harsh asceticism.

As a young nobleman, Aloysius Gonzaga led a privileged life. (Courtesy of the Institute of Jesuit Sources)

Aloysius Gonzaga leaves home in November 1585 to enter the Society of Jesus. (Courtesy of the Institute of Jesuit Sources)

Two years after making vows, the young Jesuit returned home to negotiate peace between Rodolfo, now the Marquis, and a cousin. Successful, he returned to the Roman College to continue his theological studies.

At twenty-three Aloysius summoned all his courage when the plague swept Rome in 1591. Jesuits nursing the victims were contracting the disease in alarming numbers, and Aloysius was forbidden to return to the hospitals. He begged for permission and was assigned to *La Consolazione*. Lifting a patient who was oozing pus, he turned pale and looked faint, according to a companion, but recovered his nerve and continued. On March 3 he found a sick man unconscious on the street and carried him to the hospital.

That very day illness drove Aloysius to bed. His fever raged for weeks, and he anticipated "the land...of the living...the contemplation of God." He recovered, but weakened. The slower fever of tuberculosis set in. To Robert Bellarmine, his spiritual director, Aloysius confided a premonition

of death on the octave of Corpus Christi. He dictated a letter for his mother and received the sacraments.

On the octave day, June 20, 1591, he seemed stronger until evening. As the night hours wore on, he gripped his crucifix and repeated St. Paul's words, "I wish to be dissolved and to be with Christ." Shortly before midnight, he was.

Aloysius Gonzaga was canonized in 1726 and is memorialized on June 21. He is the patron of all who care for AIDS patients.

Having found a plague victim unconscious in the street, Gonzaga carries him to a hospital.
(Courtesy of the Institute of Jesuit Sources)

Robert Bellarmine (1542-1621)

Inter-religious controversy raged in public disputations, sermons, academic lectures and books. Catholic leaders invited Robert Bellarmine to teach and preach. He argued points of theology with respect for his Protestant opponents. The times brewed bitterness; Bellarmine was effective with gentleness and good humor.

■ *Robert Bellarmine is at his desk in Rome, with a portrait of Ignatius on the wall. An artist in India made this color copy of an engraving, a process typical of the Jesuit missions. (Photo courtesy of Edward Schmidt, S.J.)*

Young Robert Bellarmine amused himself during boring classes by jotting in his notebook margins, for example, "Lectures...came to an end...the professor fell into a fever, etc., thanks be to God"; and "If the good Averroes...wants to be a beast, why let him.... But we don't!"

Later, as a teacher, he opposed the standard punishment of flogging the boys. He maintained discipline without it, despite being short.

Humor and gentleness seasoned this brilliant theologian, even as he wrestled with the other great minds of his day. At the University of Louvain he respectfully disputed an older professor's ideas. Pope Benedict XIV called him "the hammer of heretics," yet his method was not personal antagonism. While powerfully presenting his own understanding of the truth, he appreciated the ideas of Protestant writers.

His books reveal why Pope Clement VIII called him "the most learned man in Europe." One was so scholarly that readers assumed it was the work of a team. His catechism remained in use for three centuries.

At thirty-four, Bellarmine was appointed to teach at the Society's Roman College. As spiritual father of the students and as rector, he led in a spirit of service, fostering unity among 220 men from all over Europe.

■ *Bellarmine (left) and Claude La Colombière fostered awareness of Christ's love. (Detail of stained-glass window by Evie Hone, St. Stanislaus School, Dublin; Yearbook S.J. 2001, courtesy of the Society of Jesus Office of Press and Information)*

He was, successively, provincial superior of Naples, Vatican official, cardinal, archbishop of Capua and papal advisor. Bellarmine tried in vain to resist the cardinalate and wept all through the ceremony. As archbishop he lived simply and gave freely, even pawning his episcopal ring. His household steward protested when Bellarmine told him to cut up the wall hangings to clothe the poor. Bellarmine countered, "The walls won't catch cold."

As a man of deep prayer, an intimate friend of God, he loved one and all. His friend Galileo invited him to peer into the heavens through a telescope. Bellarmine respected Galileo's view of the solar system as a hypothesis but did not recognize it as fact. When a church review concluded against Galileo, the Pope sent Bellarmine to inform the scientist, gently and no doubt sadly.

Bellarmine served the Catholic Reform as a theologian and as a preacher, calling his listeners to spiritual renewal. That included popes; he denounced corruption in the papal court. When Pope Sixtus V asserted papal power over civil authority, Bellarmine opposed him. Bellarmine's argument laid the theological foundations for the separation of Church and State which would influence Thomas Jefferson in drafting the United States Constitution.

The "biggest little man in the world" died on September 17, 1621. He was buried, as he had requested, at the feet of his saintly spiritual son, Aloyisius Gonzaga. Robert Bellarmine was canonized in 1930 and declared a Doctor (teacher) of the Church. His feast day is September 17.

"Our way of proceeding"

An early leader in the Society, Jerome Nadal (1507-1580), summarized the Jesuit ideal as acting "in the Spirit, from the heart, practically." He meant referring all to God's grace, involving the feelings, and helping others.

■ *The letters IHS became the Society's emblem, symbolizing the name Jesus with its first three letters in Greek (H actually representing the Greek letter eta). (Courtesy of the Institute of Jesuit Sources)*

■ *Nicknamed "Brother Jolly" in the Belgian novitiate, John Berchmans (1599-1621) lived by the motto, "Whatever you do, do it with your whole heart and all your energy." He believed that a Jesuit's heart "must be as large as the world." A scholastic in the Roman College, he died at twenty-two. (Anonymous, Flemish, ca. 1730. In Jesuit church Aalst, Belgium. Courtesy of Archives, Province of Belgium)*

Chapter III

Embracing the Whole World

*"A good many adventurers cross the seas
to do business, spurred by earthly interest.
Can you suffer the people of the world to be more solicitous
to gather merchandise and perishable goods
than Christ's servants to rescue souls
that cost the Son of God so dearly?"*
(St. Alphonsus Rodriguez, S.J.)

Jacques Marquette

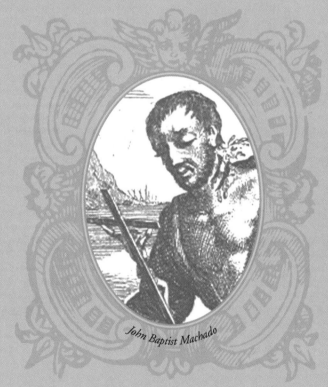

John Baptist Machado

Embracing
the Whole World

The Society's archives overflow with impassioned letters in which men pleaded with their Father General to let them pour out their lives in the missions. These well-educated European gentlemen were begging to travel thousands of dangerous miles from home and family, to live in utterly primitive conditions, to risk their lives among hostile peoples.

"Send me by your charity to China," Pedro Martinez wrote in 1560. "I have great strength and health, blessed be God, and I want to spend them both in His divine service, even to the shedding of my blood and the giving of my life." He was sent westward, the first Jesuit to set foot on North American soil. Florida's Timucuans martyred him as he clutched his crucifix.

Soldiers of fortune and merchants venture for profit. Why would Jesuits seek such perils? The answer is utter dedication to God's glory and to the eternal happiness of millions who had never heard of Jesus Christ. They would bear witness to the ultimate realities of faith and love. The stakes were life and death....death in this world, life eternal.

Besides Xavier's courage, they would need Ignatius's diplomacy to negotiate their way among European powers and the complex dynamics of indigenous peoples.

Jesuit missionaries embraced the vast world, from Asia to the Americas. They bore hardship and oppression with their flocks. They worked within the cultures they found. Forty indigenous languages were first put into writing by Jesuits crafting tools of evangelization. As they forged bonds of collaboration and community, the missionaries came to love and be loved by new brothers and sisters in Christ.

■ *(Yearbook S.J. 1999, courtesy of the Society of Jesus Office of Press and Information). Below: (Courtesy of the Institute of Jesuit Sources)*

John Francis Régis (1597-1640)

■ *John Francis Regis is pictured with his travel gear.*

As a home missioner, John Francis Regis climbed the mountains of France's Massif Central, rekindling the faith of Catholics who were spiritually starved after the long Wars of Religion.

He preached missions in the cities during the summer and in the mountains during winter, when the hard-working *montagnards* were more available. Long abandoned, they said that a saint had come to them.

In the cities Regis faced opposition from pimps, when he found honorable work for prostitutes, and sometimes from wayward priests who lied about him to the bishop. Everywhere he spoke powerfully in simple words and charitable deeds, sparking a lasting spiritual revival.

Late in 1640 Regis had a premonition of death and made a retreat in preparation. Just before Christmas he and Brother Claude Bideau, lost in a mountain snowstorm, spent the night in a freezing shed. When they reached their destination, Lalouvesc, Regis immediately began preaching and hearing confessions. Three Christmas Masses, more confessions, the draft from a broken window—all took their toll. He collapsed; pneumonia had set in. Shortly before midnight on December 31, he told Brother Bideau, "I see our Lord and our Lady opening the gates of Paradise for me."

Canonized in 1737, John Francis Regis is celebrated on July 2.

The Expanding 17th Century

A century had passed since Ignatius was born, the most exciting century of human history thus far. Two hemispheres were discovering each other.

European Catholicism was responding to its most serious challenge in centuries. Jesuits were in the forefront of its internal reform. The Society of Jesus was creating an educational system that began to circle the globe.

Jesuit zeal knew no boundaries.

Logistics, however, were entangled with European power. Rulers, merchants and conquistadores controlled travel to missionary destinations and were often at cross-purposes with the missionaries. Local politics and prejudices also came into play.

Portuguese navigators had felt their way, linking Western Europe and Asia by sea. Their settlements dotted the route from Lisbon around Africa and India to Macao on the south China coast. Yet they were barred from the interior. The Chinese assumed that anything European was inferior to their own ancient culture.

In the Americas, explorers and colonists armed with muskets overwhelmed the indigenous people. To separate their areas of influence in South America, Portugal was allotted the east coast, Spain the west. The Society established provinces in Brazil

(From Lost Paradise *by Philip Caraman, S.J. Used by permission of the Society of Jesus [British Province])*

and Peru as well as making expeditions into North America, most notably into Canada. Launched by Father Diego de Torres in 1605, the Society's Province of Paraguay stretched south of Peru, from Atlantic to Pacific.

Torres soon ran afoul of Spanish colonists. He confronted their systematic coercion of the Indians into forced labor, which was contrary to royal decrees. He marshaled the forces of law against this virtual slavery. Having freed the Indians working at the Society's college in Santiago, Chile, he paid them back wages then rehired them as employees.

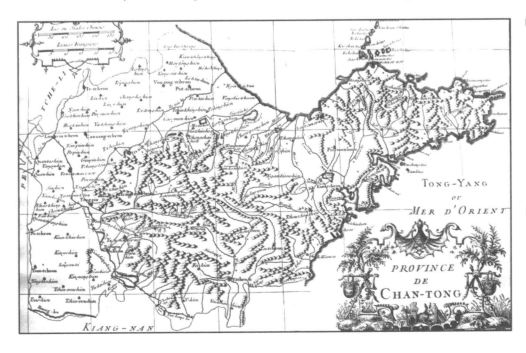

■ *(Map based on Jean Baptiste du Halde's* General Description of China).

■ *Page 47: Jacques Marquette sculpted by Ron Knepper, photo by Don Johnson, courtesy of Marquette University. Machado courtesy of the 26 Martyrs Shrine, Nagasaki, Japan. John Baptist Machado, a Portuguese, was martyred in Japan in 1617.*

His deeds inspired undying loyalty from the Indians and undying animosity from colonists greedy for unpaid labor.

The Jesuit reductions of Paraguay were born out of this tension between exploitation and justice. Torres and a sympathetic governor, Hernando Arias de Saavedra, agreed on a plan to assure the Indians' liberty and to stabilize the region east of Asunción (today's Paraguay and southern Brazil). At the invitation of the Guaraní Cacique (Chief) Arapizandú, the Jesuits evangelized nomadic tribes. They led the converts back to settlements (called reducciónes), which were places of peace. At the movement's peak, there were more than twenty reductions, with populations from 350 to 7,000.

The missionaries protected and educated the Indians and introduced them to Christ. Under the Jesuits' leadership, hunters and gatherers developed agriculture, self-government, trades and new artistic skills. Their churches rivaled Europe's cathedrals in beauty.

The reductions came to a bloody end, but that story belongs to another century.

■ *Brother Andrea Pozzo (1642-1709) told the Society's story and commemorated Jesuit saints in paintings. Art became an important means of evangelization and inspiration. (Courtesy of the Institute of Jesuit Sources)*

Claude La Colombière (1641-1682)

Born into the French nobility, the gentle Claude La Colombière entered the Society at seventeen. After an outstanding academic career which won him respect in high places, he was assigned to the obscure town Paray-le-Monial.

In its Visitation Convent, Sister (later Saint) Margaret Mary Alacoque had received visions of Jesus Christ. Misunderstood and criticized, she had heard Christ say, "I will send you my faithful servant and perfect friend." It was Claude.

Jesuit teachings had prepared him to recognize in her visions God's saving love for all, manifested through Jesus' humanity. On June 21, 1675, they privately observed the feast of the Sacred Heart, later extended to the whole Church.

La Colombière's next assignment, as preacher for the Catholic Duchess of York in anti-Catholic England, involved walking a political tightrope. Falsely accused in 1678, he grew ill with tuberculosis in prison. When released, he continued to spread devotion to the Sacred Heart in France before dying on February 15, 1682.

Canonized in 1992, Claude La Colombière is celebrated annually on February 15.

■ *Claude La Colombière preached and heard confessions for royalty and peasants.*

■ *Devotion to the Heart of Christ has marked the Society's spirituality through the centuries.*

Matthew Ricci (1552-1610)

Matthew Ricci was not the first European to enter China, not even the first Jesuit. He was, however, the first to bridge the cultural chasm. He understood that God speaks every language.

Both Chinese and Europeans clung to a sense of superiority. China closed its borders to most outsiders. Christians assumed that accepting the faith required adopting European ways.

Ricci was an apostle of Christ in the silk robes and the cultivated language of a Chinese sage.

■ *Matthew Ricci became known in China as Li Ma-tou. (Painting in the Sanctuary of Loyola, photo by Agustín Arenas. Yearbook S.J. 1996, courtesy of Society of Jesus Office of Press and Information)*

■ *Matthew Ricci and his friend and convert Hsü Kuang-ch'i
(Paul) collaborated on evangelization through literature.
(Courtesy of the Institute of Jesuit Sources)*

Matthew was born in Macerata, Italy, in 1552. It was the year of Francis Xavier's death off the coast of China. Did the boy hear about the great missionary when he enrolled in a Jesuit school at the age of nine? He kept in touch with the Society when he went to Rome for university studies in 1568, after three years of work in his father's pharmacy. Matthew entered the Jesuit novitiate in 1571 and repeatedly requested to be sent to India.

Studies came first. He loved astronomy and science and soaked up the lessons of the eminent mathematician Christopher Clavius, S.J. When classmates nicknamed Matthew "the mathematician," little did they know that this knowledge would be his instrument of evangelization.

Finally, the assignment came—to the China mission, in 1577. His studies continued in India, where he was ordained in 1580. In studying St. Thomas Aquinas he learned an essential lesson, that faith was best shared "by persuasion, and not by coercion."

Ricci had mentors in Alessandro Valignano, S.J., and Michele Ruggieri, S.J. Both endorsed what would today be called inculturation, the belief that the Gospel finds expression within many cultures and should not be imposed from outside. Matthew arrived in Macao, the Portuguese outpost on the south China coast, in 1582. Learning Mandarin Chinese proved easier for him than for most Europeans. His prodigious memory was to be a great missionary asset.

With bribes and promises, Ruggieri and Ricci gained passports to enter China. In September 1583, the two arrived in Shiuhing wearing tunics,

with their heads shaven, their appearance marking them as men of God like the Buddhist monks. The city prefect, Wang P'an, befriended them, helped them establish a house and chapel and taught them Chinese etiquette. Ricci had transformed himself into Li Ma-tou.

Shiuhing's leading citizens visited the Jesuits in curiosity, then amazement at such marvels as chiming clocks, maps, a prism and a second floor! They respected knowledge. Ricci saw the prestige he earned as a opportunity for "this initial sowing of the gospel seed."

The Jesuits remained under suspicion as outsiders and tarred with the same brush as Buddhist monks who fell into disfavor. Expulsion was always a danger. In 1589, their property was confiscated on charges that they had "a bell that chimed on its own" and practiced a new religion. Ricci and the companions who had replaced Ruggieri transferred to Suichow, where their friend Chü T'ai-su stoutly defended the Jesuits from stone-throwing neighbors. Ricci wrote a book on friendship that became a Chinese classic.

He obtained the Society's approval to dress in the hat and purple robe of a Chinese scholar, because "graduates" were more accepted than monks. His goal: to preach Christianity from inside Chinese culture.

China's rich but enclosed intellectual sphere shut out Christianity on the assumption that anything Western must be inferior. Ricci's

Missionary qualifications

While many candidates entered the Society to save their own souls, their Jesuit formation expanded their spirits with confidence and zeal. Superiors assigning missionaries used the following criteria:

The applicant for the foreign missions must be
• firm in his vocation,
• solid in his virtues,
• dedicated to prayer and discipline,
• humble and devoted to poverty and obedience, peace and charity,
• respectful of authority without any tendency to kowtow,
• zealous and willing to sacrifice for the saving of souls,
• healthy,
• effective in varied positions, including administration,
• able to learn new languages,
• friendly and outgoing,
• able to get along with people of different backgrounds,
• firm and cool, not excitable.

knowledge shook that assumption, whether he was drawing maps or translating Euclidean geometry or predicting eclipses. As he demonstrated how to derive square and cubic roots, he used truth to open doors that would also let in Christ.

Ricci longed for an interview with Emperor Wan Li in Peking (today's Beijing). He hoped to convince the Son of Heaven to permit them permanent residence and endorse their preaching. Despite plots, robbery and imprisonment, he kept trying for almost twenty years. Laden with gifts, Ricci and the Spaniard Diego Janotja finally reached the outskirts of the imperial palace in January 1601.

His chiming clock fascinated the emperor, but the Jesuit waited in vain for a personal interview. However, the emperor's enthusiasm about Ricci's maps—the first in China to illustrate the distribution of oceans and land masses—led him to grant a residence permit. (Seeing China in the middle also pleased the emperor.) Li Ma-tou was China's pre-eminent scholar!

Peking's educated mandarins responded both to Ricci's science and to his capacity for friendship. Some embraced Christianity. Chü T'ai-su recounted poetically, "My heart is opening to the light of grace like the tender bud of a fragile flower opening to the sun." Li Chih-tsao, a geographer, collaborated with Ricci on translations. Together they composed a long poem about the constellations. Li became a Christian ("Leo") on the threshold of death—then recovered and dedicated his life to God. Hsü Kuang-ch'i was a scholar baptized by Ricci as Paul. Books were the best way to spread Christianity, Paul urged. The Jesuit's writings and translations won him an enduring place in Chinese culture. Five of his treatises appear in a 1781 Chinese encyclopedia.

As superior of the Chinese Mission from 1597 on, Ricci was the leader of up to sixteen Jesuits residing in five cities. Those who lived with him testified later to the great man's humility and holiness and to his utter dedication to God's honor. By 1609 there were 2,500 Chinese Christians. There was a new Catholic church in Peking.

In 1610 Ricci's great heart and tired body began to fail. He said goodbye to his brothers and with them offered the prayers for the dying. On May 11, he died. The emperor donated a burial site for "One who attained renown for justice and wrote illustrious books."

For twenty-seven years, Matthew Ricci had been a bridge of understanding in the name of T'ien-Chu, the Lord of Heaven. The Church honors him as Servant of God.

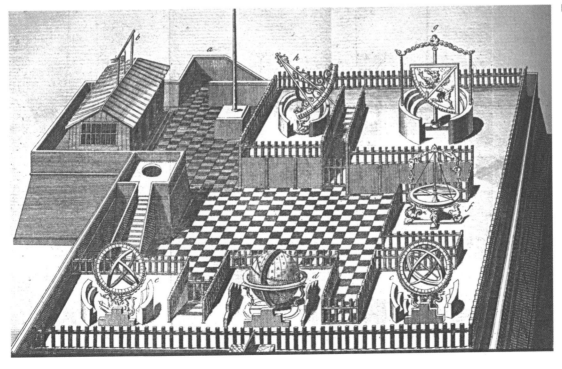

■ *The Jesuits' rooftop astronomical observatory in Peking (now Beijing) had highly developed instruments for the times. (Courtesy of the Institute of Jesuit Sources)*

Antonio Ruiz de Montoya (1585-1652)

Antonio Ruiz de Montoya was engaged in the Society's historic missionary initiative in Paraguay, the reductions. These Christian settlements offered refuge for Indians who were being hunted down by Portuguese colonists greedy for what they called "red gold," that is Indian slaves. Colonial government officials resented the reductions' tax exemptions and freedom. They accused the Jesuits of ruling a state within a state.

Raids, "molocas," became frequent. Bows and arrows were no defense against the Portuguese muskets. In 1630 alone, an estimated 30,000 Indians were either murdered or carried off as slaves. Between 1628 and 1631, over 60,000 were sold as slaves in São Paulo.

Ruiz de Montoya shared the difficult life of his people and became the voice of justice on their behalf.

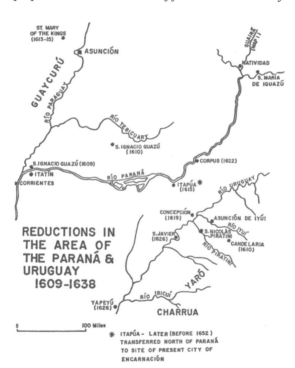

■ *(From* Lost Paradise *by Philip Caraman, S.J. Used by permission of the Society of Jesus [British Province])*

Scholars admire him as a brilliant linguist. *The Catholic Encyclopedia* calls him a man "made of cast iron." For the Church he represents solidarity with the oppressed.

Friends of the teenaged Antonio Ruiz de Montoya might not recognize these evaluations of the wild prankster they knew. His escapades were more like "juvenile delinquency." Was his daring also the ingredient of a missionary? Was the thrill-seeker also looking for something more than the world had to offer? As he tested the rules, was he learning to put law to the test of justice?

At twenty-one, Antonio wanted to see the world beyond Lima, Peru, where he had been born in 1585. In 1606 he was prepared to sail to Spain, the power-center of a vast colonial empire. At the same time, something was happening deep inside, something that he could not yet express. He confided in a friend, who suggested going to Mass. Receiving Communion was a moment of grace, one that changed his travel plans and the rest of his life. He decided to make the Spiritual Exercises with the Jesuits in Lima.

■ *Ignatius displays the Society's dedication to the name of Jesus (IHS) and "to the greater glory of God" (AMDG). This Uraguayan sculpture is reminiscent of the flourishing artistic culture in the reductions, where indigenous artists produced images of great vitality. (Yearbook S.J. 2001, Courtesy of Society of Jesus Press and Information Office)*

Alphonsus Rodriguez (1533–1617)
Peter Claver (1580–1654)

Alphonsus Rodriguez and Peter Claver are at two poles of the missionary dynamic: inspiration and action.

Rodriguez became a Jesuit brother in mid-life, after the deaths of his wife and three children and the collapse of his wool-exporting business. As doorkeeper of the college in Palma, Majorca, he impressed all with his fervor and deep prayer. His special grace was to recognize God in each person. "I'm coming, Lord," he would say when the doorbell rang.

The student Peter Claver sought out the doorkeeper for spiritual conversation; "my saintly master" he called Brother Alphonsus. Rodriguez repeatedly urged him to go to New Granada (now Colombia) to "rescue souls" among Native Americans. Claver did so and discovered the plight of Africans enslaved and transported to Cartagena for sale. He signed his solemn profession document "Peter Claver, ever a slave of the Africans."

Whenever a slave ship was sighted, Claver rushed to the port with one of his African interpreters, his beloved collaborators. One, Calepino, knew eleven languages. In the ship's hold, they gently offered comfort, food and care to the terrified captives, then accompanied them to holding sheds. The Jesuit catechized and baptized "a little over 300,000." Wealthy citizens were irritated to discover that they had to wait in line with slaves to make their confessions.

Alphonsus Rodriguez experiences a vision of Mary and Jesus. (Courtesy of the Institute of Jesuit Sources)

"Look for God in all and serve them as images of him," Rodriguez had counseled. For thirty-five years Claver lived this teaching of "my dear Alonso." In 1651 he caught the plague, followed by Parkinson's Disease. Helpless, he patiently endured a hired caregiver's neglect and abuse for four years. At his death, Cartagena's slaves lamented, "Our best friend is dead."

Alphonsus Rodriguez is memorialized on October 31 and Peter Claver on September 9. They were canonized together in 1888.

Peter Claver sought to alleviate the suffering of Africans who were being sold into slavery in Cartagena, Colombia. (Painting by James Hasse, S.J.)

In the First Week Antonio heard a call to join the Society. He was eager to go on an adventure for Christ, but as a novice he was not yet eligible for the missions.

After ordination, he began his missionary life at twenty-seven, in the new Province of Paraguay. He and Father Martín Urtasún reached the remotest part of Guairá (east of the Uruguay River in today's southern Brazil) in 1612. They described what they found there: Fathers José Cataldino and Simón Masseta, "extremely poor but rich in contentment. Their clothing consists of so much mending that hardly a trace of the original material is visible. The shoes are held together by pieces of fabric cut from their cassocks. Their hut is just like any of the Indians' huts." The new recruits participated in founding a mission for seven hundred families. They lived in "so much peace of mind and contentment that the desire to stay is almost selfish."

Ruiz de Montoya had the skills of leadership and organization to participate in developing eight more reductions. In 1620 he was appointed superior of the ten Guairá communities and soon of all the Paraguay province's missions. A true shepherd, he braved the wilderness to visit them. As a tool of evangelization, Ruiz de Montoya developed a study of Guaraní grammar, vocabulary and pronunciation, which was printed in 1640.

In September 1627, Jesuits in São Paulo sent their brothers in the reductions a warning: Portuguese *"bandeirantes"* were planning a major *moloca*. Ruiz de Montoya appealed to the authorities for protection. "Let the devil take those Indians!" was their reply.

Devastation followed, in one reduction after another. The only solution seemed to be exodus. Safety lay westward along the Uruguay River, in the reductions between it and the Paraná River. Ruiz de Montoya and Masseta led the 15,000 survivors. The people built seven hundred rafts and numberless canoes. They gathered provisions and took what little they could carry from their homes, workshops and churches.

It was a harrowing journey. Halfway down the river the refugees came to the brink of a ninety-foot waterfall. For eight days they carried rafts and canoes—everything—to the waters below the falls. Three hundred canoes had to be repaired. By the time they reached their destination, 5,000 had perished. Yet 10,000 had been saved.

Ruiz de Montoya was dispatched to Spain in 1637 on behalf of the reductions. He negotiated with officials and outmaneuvered the colonists' supporters. Passionately he appealed to King Philip IV: "My desire to obtain remedy made me travel countless miles and leaning on this staff in my hand I have come, dying, as Your Majesty can see, to the royal feet to ask for help...." He obtained royal decrees against further marauding. Delayed by war, the negotiations took six years.

The Jesuit arrived back in Lima in 1643. More negotiations kept him there until 1648. Then finally he could return to his beloved missions!

He set out but was urgently recalled to Lima. Bishop Bernardino de Cárdenas had confiscated the Society's college and missions. The bishop repeated accusations that had already been proven false—that the Jesuits had secret gold mines, that the Jesuits were heretics. Eager to get their hands on Indian slaves, colonists spread the lies. Ruiz de Montoya sought an independent commission to investigate all charges, clear the Society's name and return the institutions.

He was never able to return to his flock, but his flock came to him. When they learned of his death in 1652, forty Guaranís came to Lima to take his body home. They carried it through all the missions until they could lay him to rest in his old Reduction of Loreto. Their pastor, their companion in suffering and their champion, would be with them still.

The name of the diocesan Instituto Superior Antonio Ruiz de Montoya in Posadas, Argentina, stands for cultural solidarity and commitment to the Church's social teachings.

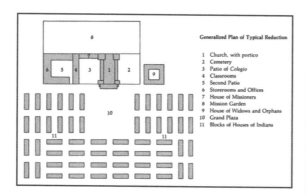

Generalized Plan of Typical Reduction

1 Church, with portico
2 Cemetery
3 Patio of Colegio
4 Classrooms
5 Second Patio
6 Storerooms and Offices
7 House of Missioners
8 Mission Garden
9 House of Widows and Orphans
10 Grand Plaza
11 Blocks of Houses of Indians

■ *Reductions were well-organized civic communities, typically centered around the church.*

Alexander de Rhodes (1591-1660)

Alexander de Rhodes's life and death were shaped by the Society's mission to east Asia, launched by Francis Xavier. With de Rhodes that mission reached Cochin-China (in modern Vietnam). His inspiration was the "great workers...filling the whole Orient with the light of the Gospel...the martyrs who are the crown of our province."

■ *Alexander de Rhodes is dressed for service in the "China mission."*

With energy and enthusiasm, with unfailing good humor, the "Apostle of Vietnam" crossed the face of the earth. When he got sleepy, he drank another cup of tea to stay awake. A man on the run has to use the nights.

Alexander de Rhodes wrote his own saga....

By twenty, he was already on the road, leaving his home in Avignon, where he had been born in 1591. His triple destination was Rome, the novitiate of the Society of Jesus and "those great lands where so many souls are perishing for lack of preachers."

The new Jesuit made a six-year assault on Father General Acquaviva, begging to be sent to Japan. In 1618, the assignment came. He sailed from Lisbon (April 4, 1619) to Goa to Cochin to Malacca to Macao (May 29, 1623).

Japan, however, had been closed to missionaries. Instead, de Rhodes, now ordained a priest, sailed with four other Jesuits in December 1624 for Cochin-China, in the southern part of today's Vietnam. He worked hard to learn the tonic language, which at first sounded to him like "the twittering of birds." He eventually composed a Vietnamese grammar, dictionary and catechism and popularized a system for writing the language in roman letters, an enduring contribution to the nation.

His chief purpose was effective preaching. The missionaries wanted to plant Christianity within the culture, preserving traditional ceremonies and customs when possible.

De Rhodes was sent north to the kingdom of Tongking in 1627, because he was "not so indispensable," he wrote, in his self-effacing manner. Actually, he spoke the language best. The Tongkinese king's fascination with a European clock bought him two years there. "Not just two years, sire," he pleaded, "but all my life."

His preaching bore fruit in hundreds, then thousands of new Christians, including members of the royal family. The newly baptized caught fire with a spirit like that of the early Church. De Rhodes was awestruck at the dedication of his catechists, mostly single young men. To them he entrusted the vibrant Christian community when, in 1630, a royal edict banished him from Tongking. Men with concubines did not like his preaching of monogamy. Neither did the concubines.

Under house arrest, he won over the landlord, who let him out the back window while the guards watched the front door. For two

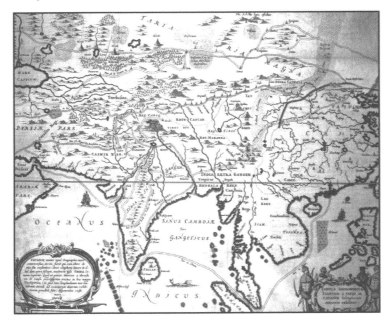

■ *(Courtesy of the Institute of Jesuit Sources)*

Protomartyr Andrew (center) is at the head of 117 martyrs of Vietnam in Song of Heroes (Thien Anh Hung Ca), *a fresco behind the altar in the Vietnamese Catholic Center (Orange County, California). Artist Hoang Pham has grouped the martyrs in an alpha (those of non-Vietnamese origin) and omega (Vietnamese). Fields of ripe rice flank instruments of their torture and death. (Photo courtesy of Trung Pham, S.J.)*

months he ministered in Christian homes at night, returning before daybreak with the guards none the wiser. When de Rhodes was deported, the ship's captain took a liking to him and let him escape by boat. He and a companion came to land only at night for ministry. Finally they were caught. "Quite disconsolate," the missionary returned to the Jesuit base in Macao, where he spent ten years as a teacher and pastor.

The Jesuits had been expelled from Cochin-China, too. But de Rhodes went there in 1640 to rebuild the ministry. His brief stay ended with the governor's order to get out "even if we had to walk on the water." In 1644 he was back again.

To lead people to eternal happiness, he faced danger and poured out his life. De Rhodes loved whole nations. But his love was not abstract; he appreciated acquaintances and gave his heart to friends. His pages are full of them: the septuagenarian judge weeping at their parting; the courageous and wise Cochin-Chinese princess Marie Magdalene; the blind Paul and his wife Monica, jointly "the soul of the church."

The brotherhood of catechists, his collaborators, gave de Rhodes his deepest joy and sorrow.

Together they faced persecution. A nineteen-year-old named Andrew was the first to receive the death penalty on a trumped-up charge, on July 26, 1644. Not yet under arrest himself, de Rhodes stayed at his side as Andrew knelt in prayer. A soldier drove a spear through the young Christian's back. It emerged "at the front.... The good Andrew looked at me very lovingly as if bidding me adieu. I told him to look to heaven...where our Lord Jesus Christ was waiting for him." The spear was pulled out and struck again. Andrew was still kneeling. A scimitar blow to the neck...then a second...severed Andrew's head. He was the first Christian martyr of Vietnam. Others would follow his brave example.

De Rhodes ministered clandestinely. Sentenced to death in early 1645, he yearned for martyrdom. When the sentence was commuted to banishment, "I could have died of misery." For the last time, "I left Cochin-China in the body, but certainly not in the heart."

After thirty years in Asia, de Rhodes was sent to Europe, with three objectives for the missions: bishops, Jesuit missionaries and funds. He journeyed west by way of Java, Celebes, India, then overland through Persia, Armenia and Anatolia. Everywhere he marveled at new sights and customs and made new friends. By June 1649 he was in Italy, enjoying reunions with his novitiate companions.

For three years he labored, mostly meeting disappointment. All the time, he longed to return to eastern Asia.

It was not to be. Eager for an overland route between Europe and the Asian missions, Father General Nickel sent de Rhodes in 1655 to Ispahan, Persia, to welcome and advise Jesuits headed eastward. The Apostle of Vietnam died in Persia on November 5, 1660.

De Rhodes's memoirs reveal a fearless man with a huge heart, naïve about marvels and shrewd about people. His vivid stories, often humorous, are always about "the ways of grace." Though convinced of the errors in other religions, he was open to the people who practiced them. He pointedly contradicted assumptions of European superiority as he described customs and institutions.

With fresh spontaneity, de Rhodes wrote his story, "wherein I have aspired to nothing...but the greater glory of God."

Jacques Marquette (1637-1675)

French exploration and colonization in North America followed the vast waterways from the Atlantic to Quebec to the Great Lakes. Tales of a great river lured explorers westward.

"Black-robed" Jesuits went far in advance of colonists, bearing Good News to the native peoples and living among them, often in the most primitive nomadic conditions and in danger of martyrdom. Inspired by the heroism of the Society's North American martyrs, French Jesuits and lay companions volunteered eagerly for the Canadian missions.

Great explorer, leader of the first European expedition down the Mississippi River, a hero of courage and endurance...whose crowning achievement was winning the hearts of Illinois villagers for Christ. This was Jacques Marquette.

Young Father Marquette burned to carry the good news where Christ's name had never been spoken. He yearned to give himself so completely as to die in the mission field. In 1668, after less than two years in Canada, he spoke fluent Algonquin. His mastery of Native American etiquette sprang from genuine fondness.

■ Père Marquette and the Indians *by Wilhelm Lamprecht, German (1838-1906). Oil on canvas 43 ¹/₂" x 53". (Patrick and Beatrice Haggerty Museum of Art, Marquette University, Milwaukee, Wisconsin)*

John de Brébeuf (1593-1649)
Isaac Jogues (1597-1646)

In allying themselves with the Hurons, the French incurred the animosity of the Iroquois, which extended to the Jesuit "Blackrobes."

John de Brébeuf was tall and strong, too large for the canoes, said the Huron traders, who called him Echon, "load-bearer." Eventually he convinced them to take him to the village of Toanché in spring 1626. Studying the language, composing a grammar and dictionary, he and his companions devoted themselves to catechesis and care for the sick. Blame was heaped on them when drought or disease afflicted

■ *Huron catechist Joseph Chiwatenwha and John de Brébeuf plan their missionary itinerary. (Drawing by Ivan Koscis, courtesy of Martyrs Shrine, Midland, Ontario)*

the village. They held themselves ready to die "in the service of our good Master Jesus Christ."

Isaac Jogues, called Ondessok, "bird of prey," by the Hurons, joined the Canadian mission in 1636. He ranged far west, but it was near Trois Rivières that he was captured by Mohawks, an Iroquois people, in 1642. His companion René Goupil was martyred. Jogues began thirteen months of enslavement in Ossernenon (now Auriesville, New York) and tortures that included gruesome mutilation of his hands. He continued to minister to his Huron fellow-captives. Jogues escaped and in France was honored as a living martyr. He returned to Canada "so that the faith could be implanted in the souls of these people."

■ *Isaac Jogues taught about Jesus by carving the sacred name on trees for his neophytes to see. (Statue at the Shrine of the North American Martyrs, Auriesville, New York. Photo by Michael Schwiegert)*

Peace with the Iroquois seemed possible in 1646. Jogues returned to Ossernenon accompanied by lay volunteer John de La Lande. He was immediately stripped and beaten, his flesh cut out and eaten. Both were beheaded.

When the Iroquois attacked Huron villages, Brébeuf and Father Gabriel Lalemant would not abandon their flock and were captured on March 16, 1649. They ran a fierce gauntlet and endured excruciating tortures and mutilations in silence. Tomahawk blows dispatched Brébeuf. Lalemant was killed the following day. The Iroquois ate both missionaries' hearts, hoping to consume their courage.

Eight North American martyrs were canonized in 1930. Their feast day is October 19.

■ *Isaac Jogues (Engraving from Matthias Tanner's book of Jesuit martyrs [1675], photo courtesy of Thomas Lucas, S.J.)*

Marquette extends his calumet, used "to put an end to disputes, to strengthen alliances, and to speak to Strangers." He came in peace. Father Jacques Marquette (1952) by Dr. Harry Wood, American (20th century). Oil on Canvas 32 1/8" x 26 1/8". (Patrick and Beatrice Haggerty Museum of Art, Marquette University, Milwaukee, Wisconsin)

"The sun shines brighter because I meet you," he told Ottawa fur traders.

At Sault-Sainte-Marie, Marquette earned the respect and affection of the Ottawa people. Next, at Saint-Esprit mission, he lived with a poor Kiskakon family, bedding down on the dirt floor among their relatives, children and dogs. He preached and nursed the sick, while planning for a mission to the Illinois people. New France's exploration of the Mis (great) Sipi (river) would be his opportunity to reach them. Though Louis Joliet officially headed the expedition, the real leader was the Blackrobe, who knew the languages and customs.

Jacques Marquette's heart beat faster on May 17, 1672, when a long-cherished dream and two fragile bark canoes launched him, Joliet and five companions into history. Marquette later documented their adventure in writing.

By June 7, at "the great village of Mascouten," they stood on the westernmost edge of the world as they knew it. Then, Marquette recounted, "We left the waters flowing to Quebec to float on those that would henceforth take us through strange lands." A week and 118 miles down the Wisconsin River, "we safely entered the Mississippi with a joy that I cannot express."

Passing through fertile prairies, they observed strange wildlife. Marquette was the first European to describe the buffalo. In one herd they counted 400 powerful beasts. Fish filled the waters. A tiger-fish violently assaulted Marquette's canoe. But no signs of human beings!

At last—human footprints on the western shore. Did they lead to welcome or to murder?

(Courtesy of the Institute of Jesuit Sources)

Marquette seized the opportunity. Perhaps he could plant the Gospel here. He and Joliet followed the path until, hearing voices, they shouted a greeting.

Amazed Illinois villagers froze at the sight of two strange figures. Eventually four elders stepped forward carrying calumets, the ceremonial pipes that symbolized peace and friendship. Marquette greeted them in the Illinois language and smoked the pipe. Their hosts honored the explorers with a banquet, and they exchanged gifts. The encounter nourished Marquette's hope for future ministry.

Downstream, they passed the mouths of the Illinois, the Missouri and the Ohio Rivers. The southern terrain bore subtropical vegetation, and mosquitoes swarmed.

Suddenly, warriors in stout wooden boats were surrounding the two small canoes. Marquette stood up and extended his calumet: "Peace!" The answer was a whizzing war-club, which barely missed him. Just in time, an elder on shore called off the warriors. Marquette tried six Native American languages in turn before communicating successfully.

At the next village, Arkamsea, they learned that the sea was only a few days' journey south, that Europeans held the river's mouth and that hostile peoples barred the way. Realizing that the sea was the Gulf of Mexico, they knew that the Europeans were Spaniards, enemies of France.

The explorers had mapped the great river and scouted potential missions. They had traveled nearly 1700 miles. On July 17 they turned back northward.

They veered northeast up the Illinois River to contact Marquette's future mission. The Kaskaskia people received him warmly, begging him to return and instruct them. Never was a promise more gladly made!

That winter Marquette fell ill at Saint-Ignace Mission. Perhaps the mosquitoes had infected him with malaria. Perhaps it was amoebic dysentery. Chills and fever consumed his strength. He could not eat and suffered dangerous diarrhea.

A bit stronger by September 1674, he set out with lay volunteers Jacques Largillier and Pierre Porteret. When his health broke down, they stopped at the southern end of Lake Michigan (present site of Chicago). Finally, they reached the new mission on April 10, 1675, Wednesday of Holy Week.

Marquette began visiting the small homes, but eager crowds made it necessary to preach outdoors. An excellent speaker and teacher, he used ten familiar objects to illustrate the Catholic faith in ten vivid lessons. Each day he taught, then celebrated the Holy Week liturgies. At last his dream had come true! He was among his people, the Illinois. He spent his meager energies in a burst of love and zeal. Easter Sunday brought the climax, the Resurrection. Fervently he celebrated what was to be his last Mass.

Marquette informed the chiefs that he had to attend an important meeting. The whole village gathered at the shore to say goodbye. Reluctant to let him out of their sight, one group followed his canoe over a hundred miles.

The missionary was operating on spiritual energy alone; his strength ebbed quickly. Largillier and Porteret were first alarmed, then desperate. They rowed obsessively, trying to return to Saint-Ignace in time to save the Jesuit's fading life. It was impossible. On a deserted spot along Lake Michigan's eastern shore, they threw up a rough bark shelter against the chill wind. They laid the joyful Marquette on the earth. At thirty-eight, his self-offering was complete—life and death in mission, no comfort except the love of God.

Take a little rest, the Jesuit urged his companions on the evening of May 18, promising to tell them when his end was near. He thanked them for their care and instructed them about his burial. Three hours later he called. As they burst into tears, he embraced and consoled them.

He asked them to hold his crucifix before his failing eyes while he professed his faith. He thanked God for the favor of dying as a member of the Society of Jesus, and a missionary, in the wilderness. Several times he exclaimed, "Jesus! Mary!" Then he looked above the crucifix, as though seeing something, and smiled.

Chapter IV
Through the Dark Valley

"My God, I do not know what must come to me today.
But I am certain that nothing can happen to me
that you have not foreseen, decreed, and ordained from all eternity.
That is sufficient for me....
I unite my sacrifice to that of Jesus Christ, my divine Savior."
(Saint Joseph Pignatelli)

Joseph Pignatelli

Jesuits endured a corporate tragedy in the eighteenth century. Like all tragedies, this drama had its victims, its villains and its heroes. At a deeper level, the suppression of the Society of Jesus between 1773 and 1814 was a corporate experience of Christ's Paschal Mystery: suffering, death and resurrection.

Dynamic, multi-faceted, well-connected, the Society had reached a peak of creative vitality and of membership. Yet in the course of a few years, thousands of Jesuits became ex-Jesuits. Many were homeless refugees. Others continued ministry as diocesan priests, chaplains, preachers or teachers.

Their disbanded educational institutions numbered 728. Of the half million books in their six hundred libraries, three quarters were sold as scrap paper.

Father General Lorenzo Ricci died in a Roman prison.

Surely many a prayer of "Why?" must have been raised to heaven, echoing the cry of Jesus on Calvary.

Yet life was never quite stamped out. The Society endured in a single province, far from its previous Roman center. It endured in pockets of brotherhood and ministry, in the quiet fidelity of its men and in silent hope.

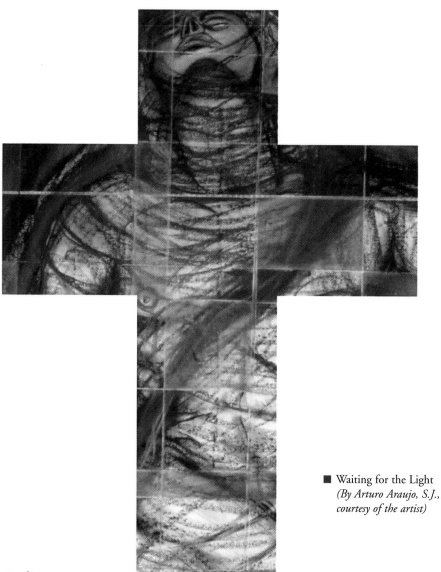

■ Waiting for the Light
(By Arturo Araujo, S.J., courtesy of the artist)

The Shadow of Death
Over the 18th Century

The Society of Jesus was a global organism by the eighteenth century, affecting and affected by the matrix in which it lived. Events in Asia and the Americas set off reactions in Europe. European national and religious struggles inflicted wounds around the world.

There were struggles aplenty. Jesuit missionaries in the Americas incurred animosity by protecting the Christian residents of their missions from forced labor for Portuguese and Spanish colonists. In Asia Jesuits worked within the cultures, offending some other missionary orders who enforced a European mode of Christianity. Complaints about the Society's methods brought Pope Benedict XIV's condemnations of the so-called "Chinese Rites" and the "Malabar Rites" in 1742.

Europe was entangled in war and revolution. As the Bourbon monarchs and others maneuvered to reduce papal power, Jesuits' loyalties fell under suspicion. Philosophers, many Jesuit-educated, led a movement titled "Enlightenment"; some of them saw reason as the antithesis of faith. They challenged absolutist monarchies and the Church. Ideas of popular sovereignty spread, especially in France, where the Church had long been a major landholder. Jesuits and ex-Jesuits felt the sharp edge of widespread anti-Catholicism.

Religious controversy was dividing Catholicism, especially in France: Jansenists vs. Jesuits. Jansenists held a rigid theology akin to Calvinism and accused the Jesuits of being lax. Blase Pascal's satires portrayed lenient Jesuit confessors forgiving unrepentant penitents; his humor reached a wider audience than the theological treatises defending the Society. At a crucial moment, 1762, France's Parlement counted many Jansenist lawyers.

Some Jesuits deserved criticism for laxity in the confessional, pride, power-grabbing, European elitism and political skullduggery. Nonetheless, the gross stereotypes of anti-Jesuit propaganda were purposeful, libelous weapons aimed at eliminating the Society entirely.

Jesuits were a powerful presence. They numbered 23,000. They were the confessors of kings, the tutors of royal households and the educators of the aristocrats and upper middle class. It might be thought that they would not go quietly. Yet the man chosen to lead was a quiet man: Father General Lorenzo Ricci. Even his best friend, Giulio Cordara, urged a strong defense. Ricci would engage in neither intrigue nor warfare, relying on the support of his friend Pope Clement XIII (1758-1769), who pledged to "fight" if the Jesuits would pray.

However, pressure was mounting for the suppression of the Society. Monarchs began to expel Jesuits from their domains: Portugal in 1759, France in 1762, Spain in 1767. Thousands upon thousands became exiles, driven from both their missions and their homelands.

When Pope Clement XIV decreed the suppression of the Society in 1773, Frederick the Great of Prussia and Catherine the Great of Russia refused to have the decree promulgated in their territories. They would not give up the educational apostolate so crucial to their countries' well-being (though Prussia eventually implemented the decree).

In Russia a remnant of the Society survived, one tree in what had once been a forest. A shoot from that tree was transplanted to Naples and Sicily in 1802. In 1814, Pope Pius VII restored the Society universally.

■ *Eusebio Kino built a chain of New World mission communities. After the Suppression of the Society, they were entrusted to Franciscan missionaries. (Mural by Nereo de la Peña in the dome of Kino's mausoleum in Magdalena de Kino, Mexico. Photo by Godehard Bruentrup, S.J.)*

Eusebio Francisco Kino (1645-1711)

With a firm colonial presence in the Americas, Spain reached northward for land, silver and forced labor. Early expeditions found inhospitable shores and desert terrain. But Jesuits dared to carry Christ's name across these dry expanses. In Mexico's Sonora Province and today's Arizona in the United States of America, the pioneer Eusebio Kino led the way.

Versatility distinguished Eusebio Francisco Kino: explorer, astronomer, cartographer, diplomat, evangelist, linguist, agronomist, rancher, builder, teacher—for the sake of the Gospel. With all these talents, he led through collaboration.

Eusebio Chini (Italian for Kühn, in Spanish Kino) was born in the Tyrol village of Segno. Illness brought him face to face with death at eighteen. When he recovered, he added Francis to his name in honor of Francis Xavier and promised to follow his new patron saint as a Jesuit, hoping to be a missionary to China. He entered the Society at twenty.

■ *Eusebio Kino. This portrait by Frances O'Brien draws upon the features of the Chino family's descendants to present Kino as faithfully as possible. (Photo by Godehard Bruentrup, S.J.)*

A brilliant mathematician at the universities of Ingolstadt and Freiburg, Eusebio was offered a full professorship. He chose instead to use his knowledge in Mexico, where he arrived in 1681.

As royal cartographer, he mapped an expedition to Baja (Lower) California in 1683. There he experienced how the Church was compromised by coming with the unwelcome conquistadors.

Kino put that lesson into practice in 1687 in founding the mission of Our Lady of Sorrows in today's Arizona. He first obtained a royal permit exempting the mission's Pima residents from servitude in the silver mines.

With his leadership the Pima people developed an agricultural center: fields, orchards, flocks and herds. They built a church, carpentry and blacksmith shops and a grain mill. They governed village affairs and administered justice. Kino's guidance was acknowledged in the saying, "The desert bloomed around him." The Jesuit began schools. To all he preached Christ. Thousands asked to be baptized.

Kino repeated this pattern, founding twenty-four missions, nineteen ranches and several towns so that the Gospel "could take root among the people" (John Paul II). Other Jesuits followed as pastors.

Being a German-speaker in a Spanish province brought him criticism, especially the charge that his mission was not properly reverential to Spain's king. Kino built an alliance with Fr. Juan Maria Salvatierra, a Jesuit official who visited and defended the mission. When the Pimas were falsely accused of violence, Spanish captains exacted harsh retribution. Kino rushed to Mexico, where all his diplomatic skills were required to restore justice for his people. He also supported the Pimas in their warfare—which he saw as defensive—with their enemies.

Kino and Salvatierra devised and negotiated a creative plan for the spiritual autonomy of Salvatierra's 1696 mission into California. They proposed that the Society of Jesus fund the expedition and have authority over the required military escort.

Kino was in the saddle constantly, making about fifty journeys of anywhere from a hundred to a thousand miles in twenty-five years. All along the way he was mapping, the first person to chart the area. He and Salvatierra proved that Baja California is a peninsula, not an island.

The last series of missions conceived by the tireless Kino would have linked Arizona and California. The project failed.

His chosen patron drew Kino across the desert again, to the pueblo of Magdalena, Sonora, in 1711. Its pastor invited the legendary dean of the mission field to officiate at the dedication of the new St. Francis Xavier Church on March 15. During the ceremony, Kino collapsed; by midnight he was dead. Commemorating the departure of a great man, the town changed its name to Magdalena de Kino.

Eusebio Kino's eminence in American pioneer history is recognized by the naming of Kino Bay on the Gulf of California, by a statue in the National Statuary Hall in Washington, D.C., and by an equestrian monument in Tucson, Arizona. The Church honors his spiritual greatness with the title Servant of God.

■ *This monumental bronze statue of Eusebio Kino in Tucson, Arizona, is one of three cast by Julián Martínez. The other two are in Segno, Italy, the pioneer padre's birthplace, and in Magdalena de Kino, Mexico, where he is buried. Citizens of Tucson, sponsored by the Arizona Historical Society, commissioned the works. (Photo by Godehard Bruentrup, S.J.)*

Costanzo Giuseppe Beschi (1680-1747)

Jesuits had been in India since Francis Xavier arrived there in 1542. Variegated Asian and European threads alternately interwove in rich new patterns or strained in conflict.

The "Father of Tamil Prose"—an Italian Jesuit! Costanzo Giuseppe Beschi so perfectly mastered this language that he is recognized as among its literary pioneers. His insertion of the Gospel into southern India followed in the great footsteps of Matthew Ricci (China) and the courageous Roberto de Nobili and John de Britto (in India before him): expressing the Good News from within the culture of their hearers.

Beschi learned Tamil quickly when he arrived as a thirty-year-old in the Madurai Mission at the subcontinent's southern tip in 1710. Nine experienced missionaries welcomed the newcomer. This mission had distinguished itself for what would today be called inculturation and kept its distance from the Portuguese colonial powers.

Within a year Beschi had transformed himself from black-robed Italian to white-robed pandaraswami, a spiritual teacher for the common people. He relished India. "God alone knows how happy I feel in this country," he wrote to Father General Tamburini. "My constitution adapts easily to this way of life so different from the one that is followed in Europe."

Besides his gift for language, Beschi brought zest, hope and a capacity for friendships and for bridging culture gaps. He welcomed challenges. Just the man to plunge into an unfamiliar world!

From village to village, he preached, instructed, baptized and gathered communities of faith. His wit and courage flashed in confrontations with challengers. Despite, or perhaps because of the success of missionaries such as Beschi, leaders in other religions felt their powerful positions threatened. Repeatedly they persecuted Christians.

In the town of Gurukelpatti, Beschi was arrested, his residence and church destroyed. The accusation was that he had contraband gold; the sentence was death. Only when a goldsmith identified the "golden" coins as brass was he freed. "The scaffold was up," he later wrote; "with a joy I have never experienced I was about to receive the

P. Robertus de Nobilibus Romanus Soc. Iesu

■ *A century before Beschi, the great Jesuit missionary Roberto di Nobili (1577-1656) had pioneered inculturation in India. He suffered opposition from outside and inside the Society. (Courtesy of the Institute of Jesuit Sources)*

palm of martyrdom." He felt deprived of "this supreme happiness" by his release. Banished from the town, he had at least the joy of knowing that the Christian community remained strong. Not a single one deserted the Faith.

The shepherd protected his sheep. In 1733, he went out to face Mughal soldiers who were threatening his parishioners in the village of Tiruchirapalli. He was taken hostage, but the commander, Chanda Sahib, freed him. The two leaders became life-long friends, and the Mughal protected the Jesuit and his mission.

Warfare occasionally made it impossible for the missionary pastor to travel his huge territory. These interludes became opportunities. He began to give the Spiritual Exercises, studied the complexities of Tamil poetry and wrote many works to advance the mission. For his catechists Beschi wrote training manuals, grammars and dictionaries and founded a school of Tamil literature and language. His long poem about St. Joseph was the first epic in Tamil.

Some of his Jesuit brethren criticized Beschi as lacking prudence. They contended that he enjoyed the company of powerful people too much and gave lavish gifts. After his protector Chanda Sahib died, Beschi was transferred to Tuticorin on the Fishery Coast in 1742, then to the college of Ambalakat. There he died on February 4, 1747.

■ *Saju George, S.J., explores the harmonies between Christian and Hindu spirituality through traditional dance. This dance posture depicts the Hindu God Vishnu reclining on the serpent in the milky ocean, eternally at rest preserving His creation. (Photo courtesy of Saju George, S.J.)*

Anthony Lavalette (1708-1767)

Jesuits played a high-stakes game at the court of France's King Louis XV—royal confessors at the center of power. By opposing Louis' mistress, Madame de Pompadour, they earned her undying hatred. Her powerful supporters allied themselves with Parlement, among whom were many of the Jesuits' Jansenist opponents. Into these hands, Antoine Lavalette's case delivered the Society's French Province.

Talent, intelligence, creativity—hallmarks of Jesuit service. In Anthony Lavalette these great possibilities turned sour. He chose to operate as a lone wolf. He served himself. The results brought ruin to him and to the Society.

Newly ordained, Lavalette arrived in French Martinique, an island of the Lesser Antilles, in 1742. The young pastor's charm and administrative abilities won admiration. No doubt his helpfulness and interest in people were sincere. But his Jesuit superiors were concerned that he was too self-confident and gave "priority to temporal over spiritual concerns." One wrote to Father General that Lavalette needed a "prudent

superior to...rein him in." Another said, "His qualities have not reached maturity."

His popularity and business acumen outweighed prudence, however, and Lavalette was appointed superior in 1753. He remained treasurer too; the Society's dire financial situation in Martinique required the genius of this son of a commercial family. Lavalette set to work. First he renovated houses and bought others, to rake in rental income. Devoting land to cash crops such as sugar, coffee, indigo and cacao, he operated plantations. He added a lucrative sideline changing money, in violation of church law.

This was all very astute. But it was not the mission of the Society of Jesus. Lavalette was living on the edge, both with the Society and with the French government.

Suddenly, a cataclysmic year of hurricanes, epidemic, piracy and war devastated his undertakings. Bankruptcy! Debt of 3,000,000 pounds! Alarmed, the French Provincial tried to control the spiraling disaster. Lavalette's response was no response. He cut off communication with his

superiors, deceived his local brothers and set up business on his own as Ranchon, Cartier & Company. He started buying products from nearby islands and selling to the Dutch—foreign trade, clearly illegal. Reports reached France.

When the Provincial refused to pay off Lavalette's debts, seeing them as personal, one creditor, Madame Grou, sued and won in 1760. What began as a financial case spilled over into condemnations of the Society's very existence. Enemies escalated a full attack, and by August 1762 the Society of Jesus was banned from France and all its territories.

Meanwhile, a Provincial Visitor, Fr. François de la Marche, had arrived in Martinique in March 1762. He confronted Lavalette before seven other Jesuits. Lavalette sidestepped the truth. Faced with documentary evidence, he acknowledged, "I no longer deny.... You want me to leave; I shall do so willingly." But Lavalette postponed his departure, allegedly to explain his complex business matters to his successor.

Lavalette schemed instead, organizing protests and pressures that endangered de la Marche. The Visitor declared him under interdict, an outcast until Father General would absolve him. His half-hearted repentance was mixed with excuses that his guilt was due to "a kind of accident." Before sailing for Europe, he decided to leave the Society.

After two years in Amsterdam, supported by a gift and pension from the Province, in 1764 Lavalette moved to Toulouse, where he repudiated the Society by taking the oath for "former...Jesuits who wish to recover the citizen's status and rights." Returning to his birth name, Valette, he lived as a recluse, glimpsed occasionally walking in the neighborhood. He died on December 13, 1767.

Dominic Zipoli (1688-1726)

If talent is a ticket to success, young Dominic Zipoli was on his way. His gift was music.

With a scholarship grant from Duke Cosimo de Medici, he studied in Naples with the great Alessandro Scarlatti. Was he a headstrong pupil? Dominic quarreled with Scarlatti and left for Bologna, then Rome, where he studied with Bernardo Pasquini. He had reached the center of Baroque creativity. He composed keyboard sonatas which are still appreciated.

Zipoli was hired as choirmaster at the Gesù and taught at the Roman College. In 1716 he entered the Society, and his ambitions turned to ministry and mission. He soon volunteered for Paraguay.

As Brother Domingo in Córdoba, Paraguay, he led the college choir, played the organ and composed choral and instrumental works. Guaraní culture treasured music, and Jesuits had long used songs as catechetical aids. Beautiful and solemn liturgies also appealed to the Guaraní soul. Performed throughout the reductions, Brother Domingo's compositions entranced a visitor, who claimed, "There can be nothing sweeter nor more elaborate than his perfect harmony."

Success did come to Dominic Zipoli, serving the greater glory of God and the good of souls.

Lorenzo Ricci (1703-1775)

Pressure was building for the Society's suppression. In 1759 Portugal began the process of closing Jesuit colleges, confiscating properties and imprisoning or expelling over 1400 members. The high-profile trial of the Jesuit Gabriele Malagrida by the Inquisition ended with his public hanging and burning in Lisbon in 1761. France (with Sicily) and Spain moved in the 1760s, first in back rooms and eventually with expulsions and the elimination of the Society at home and in Asia and the Americas.

The election of Pope Clement XIV in 1769 spelled doom. He had let it be known that a Pope could dissolve any religious order. He dissolved the Society in 1773.

Disaster extracts either the best or the worst from those crushed in its winepress. Lorenzo Ricci responded to betrayal and persecution not with bitterness but with integrity and demands for justice.

The Society called Lorenzo Ricci to leadership in its darkest hour. Instead of a military general to lead them into combat, in May 1758 the General Congregation elected a candid, humble man. As the balloting turned his way, he hid in the Gesù church loft. Like Jesus in Gethsemani, he prayed, "Let this chalice pass from me." Calvary awaited him.

Ricci came to the fray from a theology professorship and experience as a spiritual director. Neither training nor personality fitted him for battle. Instead he led from his own place of strength. If power politics had played a role in the hatred directed against the Society, he exemplified meekness. If pride had blinded some members, he offered humility. Ricci confronted a distinguished Jesuit preacher who had delivered a self-congratulatory sermon on the Society and tore up his text.

Bit by agonizing bit, the Society was being dismembered. Father General tried to organize the thousands of homeless Jesuits, finding them refuge and raising money for their necessities.

Ricci paid a respectful visit to the new Pope, Clement XIV. It was the last time he was allowed into the papal presence. Previously their friend, Clement was distancing himself from the Jesuits as political pressures pulled the noose ever tighter.

About 8 p.m. on August 16, 1773, there was a knock at the door of the generalate. Two papal officials, several soldiers and a lawyer demanded to see Ricci. The lawyer read a papal decree suppressing the Society of Jesus. "Do you accept this?" Father General was asked. Ricci replied that the Pope's decisions did not require his consent. Twenty-four hours later, he was arrested and interrogated.

His questioners were concerned chiefly about whether the supposedly crafty Jesuits had a back-up plan to remain in existence. "Have you chosen a successor?" they wanted to know. He had once considered Fr. Ignatius Rombergh but had abandoned that intention after the suppression. Nonetheless, Ricci told the full truth. Rombergh knew nothing of this; he must have been surprised to be imprisoned for the crime of having been thought of.

■ Waiting a Long Time
(mixed media) By Arturo Araujo, S.J. (Courtesy of the artist)

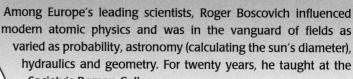

Roger J. Boscovich (1711-1787)

Among Europe's leading scientists, Roger Boscovich influenced modern atomic physics and was in the vanguard of fields as varied as probability, astronomy (calculating the sun's diameter), hydraulics and geometry. For twenty years, he taught at the Society's Roman College.

Boscovich's multi-faceted brilliance and intellectual integrity bridged national and religious divides. The Royal Society of London inducted him in 1761. Only he was able to persuade Pope Benedict XIV to remove Copernicus from the Index of Forbidden Books. Born in (today's) Dobrovnik, Yugoslavia, he crisscrossed Europe at the request of Father General Ricci as Visitor of the Society. He supervised the draining of Rome's marshland and was consulted on architectural problems with St. Peter's dome, Milan's cathedral belfry and the Austrian imperial library.

After the Society's suppression, he served as captain of optics in France's navy.

A lunar crater is named in honor of Boscovich.

The huge round bastion of Castel Sant'Angelo may look picturesque today, dominating the approach to Vatican City across the Tiber River. It was a cold, harsh prison for Lorenzo Ricci. On half rations, he had trouble eating even that pittance in the winter, his teeth chattering in the frigid air. Constant stomach pain accompanied his hunger. Even worse was the isolation. Brother Francesco Mariani was permitted to visit, but an ever-present armed guard assured that no news passed between them.

A papal commission tried to pull a veneer of law over injustice by conducting a secret trial. Ricci's detractors claimed that he deserved to be burned alive. Interrogators probed whether he had any foreknowledge of the suppression—"only public rumors"—or had stashed money or furniture in secret hiding places—"no money; no hiding places."

Why had he been arrested? Why was he in prison? Ricci demanded to know. No answer was given. When his trial failed to demonstrate any criminal activity, it was declared null and void, and the process began again.

On the morning of September 22, 1774, Rome's thousands of church bells were tolling. The prisoner was told that France's king had died (on May 10). It was not hard for Ricci to deduce that the deceased was really Pope Clement. Would his death open a path of hope?

Pope Pius VI, elected in February 1775, was eager to release Ricci but acted slowly. His strategy was to use official channels, making it clear that he was correcting an injustice, not bestowing a pardon. Ricci put his case to Pius in a letter, asking the reason for his imprisonment, a verdict in his trial, or that he be set free. The letter was intercepted and never reached the Pope.

Ricci's second year in the Castel cell rolled into a third. An icy November wind penetrated his thin and weakened frame. Among fifteen prison officials and soldiers, Brother Orlando was the only Jesuit at the dying man's bedside when he received Holy Communion for the last time. Ricci had written a final testimony and spoke it aloud. He once more declared his innocence and his trust in God. On November 24, 1775, death at last set him free.

Distressed that he had not accomplished Ricci's liberation in time, Pius VI insisted on a solemn, public funeral. Ricci was buried near the previous Fathers General, in the Church of the Gesù.

Martyrs of the French Revolution

Two decades after the Society was outlawed in France and sixteen years after the papal decree of suppression, the French Revolution exploded at the Bastille Prison on July 14, 1789.

Former Jesuits continued to minister in France as diocesan priests. They were among the clergy required to swear an oath accepting the Civil Constitution of the Clergy, which subjected the Church to the government. In November 1790, the National Constituent Assembly configured dioceses by civil departments. Bishops and priests were to be elected by citizen (not necessarily Catholics) who had sworn loyalty to the Revolutionary constitution. By November 1791, priests who refused to take the oath were subject to arrest.

If the suppression of the Society left Jesuits homeless, the bloodbath that was about to soak France would take lives. At least twenty-eight former Jesuits were among the many thousands to die in the Reign of Terror. Some were guillotined, others torn apart by angry mobs. Still others starved or succumbed to disease in prison.

Like many other French priests, Alexander-Charles-Marie Lanfant (b. 1726) had refused to take the oath. He had been the preacher for the royal household of King Louis XVI and had evoked the admiration even of the Jesuit-educated Enlightenment philosopher Denis Diderot, who remarked after hearing him, "With a sermon like this it becomes difficult not to believe." Lanfant's service to royalty made him a marked man. When he needed to hide, a Parisian bookbinder named Leriche welcomed him.

Spies sniffed Lanfant out, and he was arrested on August 29, 1792. It was front-page news in *Le Moniteur Universel* on August 31. Two days later a mob made its way to his prison. Running neck-and-neck with the angry citizens was a priest named Monnel, who had contacts among the new authorities. Just in time, he shoved into the hand of the crowd's leader a safe-conduct order for Lanfant. Spared! That bloody night saw many other priests massacred.

The next morning, September 3, Monsieur Leriche found Father Monnel and delivered the

■ *John Carroll, first Archbishop of Baltimore and first bishop of the United States of America, was a Jesuit until the Suppression. He returned to his native land to build up the fledgling church. This portrait by Rembrandt Peale (ca. 1809) is at the Basilica of the Assumption which he built, the Mother Church of American Catholicism. (Collection of the Archdiocese of Baltimore)*

news of more threats against Lanfant. Having been thwarted, the mob insisted on his head. Once again Monnel was able to obtain a reprieve, this time a release order. An hour later, Lanfant emerged from the prison. He limped through the streets, trying not to be noticed. When some pedestrians on Buci Street recognized him, they cheered for his safety. Their celebration attracted fatal attention; Lanfant was rearrested and reimprisoned.

The mob stormed the prison again on September 5. According the prison register, Lanfant was "judged by the people and executed at once."

A new priest-hunt opened in 1793, enhanced by a sizeable reward for anyone who had a priest arrested. Hundreds were condemned to deportation, but it proved impossible. In April 1794 two slave ships in the port of Rochefort, the *Deux Associés* and the *Washington*, were loaded with this human cargo and stood off-shore. Life below-decks was barely life, lacking breathable air, drinkable water and edible food. Soon typhoid fever began to release the men from this living hell.

An ex-Jesuit was among the 400 priests packed onto the *Deux Associés*. Joseph Imbert (1719-1794) had served among the diocesan clergy and as the vicar-general of the Diocese of Moulins until his arrest on June 9, 1793. With his unquenchable spark, he redirected the Revolution's anthem, "The Marseillaise," by composing new lyrics for it, to express priestly ideals. "The Priests' Marseillaise" must have lifted the spirits of his fellow-prisoners. He succumbed to typhoid fever on June 9, 1794, and was buried on the Atlantic-coast island of Aix with another 226 priests.

John Nicholas Cordier (1710-1794) put up a vigorous opposition to the Civil Constitution of the Clergy. It was no surprise when he was placed under house arrest in October 1793. On June 19, 1794, he was boarding the *Washington* at Rochefort. Its Captain Gilbert took away the old man's cane and shoved him, yelling, "You criminal!" Then Gilbert struck the 84-year-old Cordier with his sword to make him walk. Cordier was among the very ill prisoners whom Captain Gilbert eventually put off onto the Madame Island, where a makeshift hospital was set up. He survived until September 30.

Blessed Alexander-Charles-Marie Lanfant, Blessed Joseph Imbert and Blessed John Nicholas Cordier are commemorated on January 19 with other Jesuit martyrs.

Joseph Pignatelli (1737-1811)

Spain followed Portugal and France in outlawing the Society within its borders (2746 banished Jesuits) and colonial empire (2630 banished). The plan was to exile them to the Papal States in Italy. Pope Clement XIII, however, refused to recognize the banishment decree as legitimate and for over a year would not accept the exiles.

After the suppression, a remnant of the Society survived in Russia; some of these Jesuits were invited to Parma, then to Naples and Sicily. Napoleon's policy of eliminating religious bodies of all sorts struck Jesuits in Parma (1802), Bologna (1804), Naples and Sicily (1806), then Rome (1809).

Joseph Pignatelli's noble spirit built a bridge for the Society across a dark valley to a future of new life. He put his all into the service of his brethren.

■ *Joseph Pignatelli (Courtesy of the Institute of Jesuit Sources)*

Joseph and his brother Nicholas walked away from positions of eminence to join the Society. Their parents belonged to illustrious families of Naples and of Spain. Their eldest brother, the Count de Fuentes, became Spain's ambassador to Paris. Despite poor health, Joseph assisted prisoners on death row besides teaching in grammar school. His was a humble role.

He was sound asleep in the early hours of April 3, 1767, when soldiers surrounded the Jesuit school in Saragossa, Spain. The community awakened to a summons: "to the dining room!" There they were held under guard for twenty-four hours, then paraded out of town. That quickly Jesuits were refugees, by the hundreds. Their students hid in roadside hedges, stepping out to say tearful good-byes. "We could not control ourselves before so much affection," Pignatelli later recounted.

Pignatelli was among hundreds loaded onto thirteen ships on May 1. What should have been a brief voyage turned into more than a year of wandering. One port of call after another turned the ships away. After a few miserable months in Corsica, the Jesuit cargo—now 1600—was again loaded aboard, then dumped ashore in September 1768 near Genoa. From there the exhausted men, many elderly, covered 300 mountainous miles by foot and donkey to the Papal States, where Pignatelli negotiated their settlement.

He was only twenty-nine years old when the Spanish axe fell, yet the Provincial of Aragon deputed the young man to act with the Provincial's authority during the emergency. For Pignatelli, authority meant service. His mission was to support the 600 members of his province and to represent them with the ship's captains and other officials. In brief stays on land, he organized the search for food and shelter. Time and again, officials offered the Pignatellis, "Princes of the Holy Roman Empire," comfortable quarters. Joseph and Nicholas always declined, preferring to share the flea-bitten lot of their Jesuit brothers.

After the Society's suppression in 1773, Pignatelli had time for art and study during a forced retirement in Bologna. Bit by bit he gathered a small library and made it available to other ex-Jesuits, keeping contacts alive.

Nicolas, however, broke his heart, running up huge debts through luxurious living, becoming unbalanced and landing in jail for a month in 1785. Almost two decades of estrangement ended when Joseph learned that Nicholas was ill in Venice and rushed to his brother's deathbed. Tearfully they begged pardon of one another. Nicholas died in Joseph's arms.

Suppression and Restoration of the Society of Jesus

1759 – Jesuits expelled from Portugal.

1762 – Jesuits abolished in France.

1767 – Jesuits expelled from Spain.

1773 – Pope Clement XIV suppresses the Society with the brief "Dominus ac Redemptor," promulgated August 16.

1773 – Catherine the Great of Russia and Frederick the Great of Prussia refuse to have the decree of suppression proclaimed.

1775 – Pope Pius VI consents silently to the situation in Russia; Lorenzo Ricci dies.

1780 – Stanislaus Czerniewicz (Vicar-general in Russia) opens a novitiate in Russia.

1783 – Pope Pius VI orally approves the Society's continued existence in Russia.

1801 – Pope Pius VII formally approves the Society as it exists in Russia.

1802-1806 – Vicar-general Gabriel Gruber welcomes former Jesuits to reunite with the Society existing in Russia, creating a partial restoration with novitiates opening in England (1803), Dyneburg, White Russia (now Daugavpils, Latvia) (1804) and the USA (1806).

1802-1805 – The Society is restored in Naples, then in Sicily.

1806-1810 – Napoleonic forces suppress religious groups (including the Society) in Italy.

1814 – Pius VII restores the Society universally with the decree "Sollicitudo Omnium Ecclesiarum," promulgated August 7 in a chapel attached to the Church of the Gesù.

Pignatelli was asked to serve as novice master there. Twenty-three and a half years after the suppression, he renewed his vows, linked with the Russian remnant, in 1797

Once again, he was a Jesuit!

Once again Pignatelli held authority as service, first as novice-master and then Provincial for Parma. He was sent to Naples, where King Ferdinand had requested ex-Jesuits to open schools, but under diocesan authority, not as the Society of Jesus. Under cover of visiting his sister, the Countess of Acerra, Pignatelli negotiated quietly but firmly. At last Ferdinand and Pope Pius VII agreed to restore the Society in Naples and Sicily.

"Te Deum!" shook the rafters on December 3, 1802, the day of the Society's solemn return to Naples' Gesù Church. As Provincial, Pignatelli welcomed former members of the Neapolitan Province and survivors of other provinces. They preached, taught, heard confessions, directed retreats, visited hospitals and prisons.

Briefly.

Napoleonic forces invading the Kingdom of Naples in 1806 expelled all foreign Jesuits. Again Pignatelli was a refugee, again responsible for his brethren. He arrived in Rome and paid a visit to the Pope. Having stayed strong for so long, he suddenly burst into tears. Then he pulled himself together and set about serving his seventy-plus exiles. They lived quietly and simply, ministering without pay, trusting divine Providence.

Pignatelli took small but steady steps toward a public presence. The Jesuits preached missions in the countryside, conducted a school in Tivoli and a seminary in Orvieto. He formed communities and welcomed young Jesuits to tertianship, the last stage of Jesuit formation. At the Church of Good Counsel, Jesuits heard confessions and offered Mass.

Then Napoleon annexed Rome too. The Jesuits went about incognito, but some were arrested. Pignatelli helped sustain each one. When police officers occasionally burst into his residence, he received them graciously and somehow avoided deeper scrutiny.

With no income, Pignatelli always had the cash that was needed and enough to be generous. "Too generous," Brother Grassi told him.

Pignatelli was leaning on his cane and on Brother Grassi's arm as they strolled in the neighborhood on All Souls Day, 1811. They carried coins to distribute along the way. Brother Grassi later described himself as "rather stingy" and quoted the Provincial as repeating, "Come on, give, man, give." Pignatelli then took over and handed out coins more freely.

Two weeks later Joseph Pignatelli died peacefully. He had weathered almost forty-five years of exile, persecution and suppression. His diplomacy had led the Society to the threshold of full restoration.

Pope Pius VII restored the Society of Jesus universally in 1814.

Joseph Pignatelli was canonized in 1954. His feast day is November 14.

Chapter V
Confronting Modernity

"We come to your presence anguished and afflicted by the evils we witness."
(Father General Peter Beckx, Act of Consecration
of the Society to the Sacred Heart, 1872)

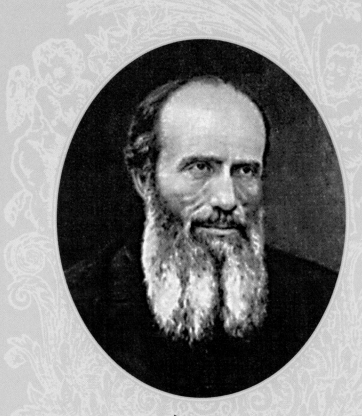

Jacques Berthieu

Confronting Modernity

The Society of Jesus was formally restored in 1814 after a near-extinction of forty-one years. Under the "second founder," Father General Jan Roothaan, it launched into education and evangelization with all the zeal of its predecessors.

Jesuits still faced animosity and often reacted defensively against contemporary ideas and movements. The Society had come back to life in a radically different era; liberalism and emerging democracies frequently exhibited anti-religious elements, and Jesuits countered by allying themselves with monarchies and with the Papacy. Political hostility and anti-Catholic sentiment exiled them from country after country of Europe, Africa and Latin America. The secular and democratic United States of America, however, became a fertile field.

Waves of fresh missionary energy once again circled the globe with schools, colleges and mission stations. Jesuits were now linked with the early Society not by oral tradition—that line had been broken—but by study of the founding documents, especially the Spiritual Exercises and the *Ratio Studiorum*. The result was a more formalized Society with well-organized, highly centralized structures.

The restored Society laid the foundations of great institutions, especially for education in the United States. For a Church on the defensive, these served as bastions of faith.

Meanwhile, sons of Ignatius continued to seek God's will and to serve "the good of souls."

Perhaps nowhere did cultures conflict so dramatically as in the American West. Caught in the tension between secular and religious dynamics, Peter John De Smet is pictured at Fort Vancouver in 1859 with (left to right, front row) Victor, Kalispell tribe; Alexander, Pend d'Oreille; Adolphe, Flathead; Andrew Seppline, Cœur d'Alene; (back row) Dennis, Colville; Bonaventure, Cœur d'Alene; De Smet; Francis Xavier, Flathead. (Photo courtesy of St. Louis University Archives)

The Modern World
of the 19th Century

"Modernity," already a reality before 1800, flowered in the nineteenth century with full-blown industrialization, science and ideals of popular sovereignty. Each development challenged long-held concepts while opening unimagined possibilities.

Technology advanced, but often at the expense of humanity, especially the humanity of workers caught in the factory system. Karl Marx conceived of a workers' revolution, a socialist utopia that was to arise out of conflict, purified of religion.

The sciences opened new insights into the world and the human person. The monk Gregor Mendel and Charles Darwin recognized the process of biological evolution. Later, Sigmund Freud and others applied scientific perspectives to human behavior.

Advances moved at such a pace that philosophical and theological understandings could not keep up, and some concluded that faith and reason must be incompatible. The Enlightenment's influence continued to place reason in opposition to faith, and certain secular states directly persecuted religion. Stripped of political power by Italy's nationalist movement, by 1870 the Papacy was confined to Vatican City. The besieged Catholic Church responded with strong central control, solidified in the actions of Pope Pius IX and the First Vatican Council (1869-1870).

In Asia, Latin America and parts of Africa, ideals of national independence clashed with European colonialism. To these same regions, missionaries carried Christian faith, often wrapped in European ways.

Social and political unrest and poverty swelled migrations, mostly to the Western Hemisphere. As peoples of vastly different worldviews encountered one another, the clash of cultures was acute.

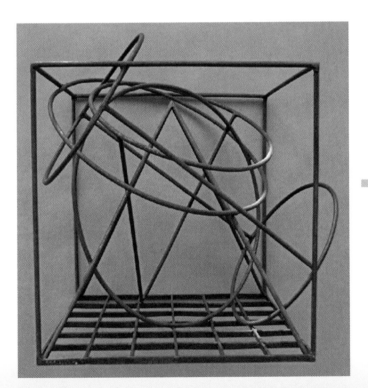

■ Cuerpo y Alma *(Body and Soul)* was sculpted by Dennis Leder, S.J., of the Universidad Rafael Landívar, Guatemala. "My being seeks for meaning," says Leder, "for spiritual issues, for authentic *meaning.*" *(Photo courtesy of the artist)*

Peter John De Smet (1801-1873)

Millions of buffalo populated North America's Great Plains in 1840, hunted by those who depended on the great animals for almost every necessity. By 1870, the buffalo were slaughtered, forts dotted the upper Missouri River, and the once-proud people were destitute. Their history and that of the Society's Missouri Vice-Province intersected.

"I always miss something when I am not among my good Indians.... I come again to my dear Rocky Mountains. Then...only am I happy." A Fleming from Europe's Low Country had found his heart's true home.

Peter John De Smet had left his native Flanders in 1821 to become a Jesuit missionary in North America. His dream was long deferred. Sick and discouraged, he left the Society from 1835 to 1837.

Pierre-Jean De Smet, S.J., Famous Indian Missioner (1869) *by George C. Eichbaum (1837-1919). Oil on canvas. Collection of the Western Jesuit Missions (Photo by David Suwalsky, S.J., courtesy of the Saint Louis University Museum of Art)*

However, Flatheads persistently seeking a Blackrobe to speak to them of the Great Spirit launched De Smet's missionary life in April 1840. "I wept for joy in embracing them, and with tears in their eyes they welcomed me with tender words."

Peter John De Smet (Courtesy of the Institute of Jesuit Sources)

"Our ears are open, our hearts will heed your words," promised Flathead Chief Big Face.

De Smet and Father General Jan Roothaan shared a vision: to replicate the Paraguayan reductions, fully integrated communities of faith and culture safe from the intrusions of Euro-American exploitation. De Smet convinced the Flatheads to establish stable residences and to learn agriculture and skills for a future when the buffalo would disappear before the inevitable westward push of whites. From St. Mary's Mission on the Bitterroot River, he wrote, "I hear the joyful voices of carpenters, re-echoing to the blows of the smith's anvil, and I see them engaged in raising the house of prayer."

■ *A mission in the Rocky Mountains (Courtesy of the Institute of Jesuit Sources)*

On horseback and by boat, De Smet and his interpreters visited the Flatheads, Pieds-Noirs, Crows, Cheyennes, Nez-Percés, Snakes, Cœur d'Alènes, Spokanes, Kettles and Sioux. He relished the open air, the varied terrain. His itineraries (over 5000 miles between April and October 1842) are breathtaking: up the Missouri River, into today's Dakotas, Montana, Idaho, Washington and Oregon.

Christmas Midnight Mass of 1844 opened in St. Ignatius Mission with carols in the Pend d'Oreille language. "Here, indeed, the Indian missionary...obtains his strength, his courage, his zeal to labor to bring men to the knowledge of the true God, in spite of...the privations of every description, and the dangers."

De Smet's loving respect for Native Americans, his willingness to share their lives and customs, won him and the Gospel a welcome. He presented Christ's message in their context.

Like Francis Xavier, he was on the move; other Jesuit priests and brothers followed to provide pastoral care at the missions of St. Ignatius, Sacred Heart, St. Francis Xavier, St. Paul, St. Peter, St. Francis Regis, Assumption, Immaculate Conception, St. Anne.... The founder, a robust

■ *De Smet preaches to a Sioux congregation during Mass. (Courtesy of St. Louis University Archives)*

outdoorsman, perhaps did not appreciate his brethren's hardships and isolation.

With little sense of frontier distances and pace of growth, Roothaan worried that the program was moving too fast. He received complaints that the missionary was on the road too much, spending too much time with lay people. Roothaan reassigned De Smet in 1848 to assist the superior in St. Louis. Without his leadership, the missions began to flounder. There had not been enough time to strengthen the mission societies for withstanding the onslaught ahead.

From his desk job, De Smet assisted and advised the missions and frequently received "very pressing invitations from them." His financial management, fund-raising and recruiting were so effective that his superior William Murphy reported, "The Vice-Province owes him almost all

it has." Father General Beckx honored De Smet with permission to make solemn vows without the standard preparation.

Gold-seekers were lobbying for a road to the Pacific coast. De Smet had mixed feelings about the Fort Laramie Treaty of 1851, which would allow free passage of whites across the plains, restricting native peoples and disrupting the migrations of the buffalo and their hunters. He wanted to trust the government negotiators, yet he recognized that the treaty "had been prepared beforehand," in Washington.

De Smet was asked to map the territories, which he knew better than anyone else. He did so in the hope that the arrangement would contribute to "a period of peace and justice" for the land's First Peoples. Only "a period." Gone was his vision of an undisturbed homeland.

Wa-tom-i-ka – James Chrysostom Bouchard (1823-1889)

Wa-tom-i-ka, "Swift-foot," was the son of Delaware Chief Kistalwa and Marie Elizabeth Bucheur/Beshard. Growing up on the Delaware reservation (in today's Kansas, USA), he loved to tell other children about the Great Spirit.

After his father's death in war, the young man was taken to a college in Marietta, Ohio, where he studied for the Presbyterian ministry. Hearing Jesuit Arnold Damen preach to children, Bouchard was drawn to Catholicism. He entered the Church in 1846 and the Society in 1848, the first Native American of the Great Plains to do so.

Much later, as United States policies evoked "anguish and...burning tears," he wrote, "O Justice, how little art thou known in this proud, boasting nation! Such is the sentiment of a poor wandering Delaware, Wa-tom-i-ka."

In 1861 Father Bouchard was assigned to California as a preacher. A familiar figure in both towns and mining camps, he lived up to his middle name honoring the ancient "golden-mouthed" saint. Yet his racist attitude toward Chinese immigrants was a curious blind spot.

"For thirty years, he had preached and taught until the people of California, Oregon, Nevada and the territories beyond the Sierras had come to love and venerate his name," recalled New York's *Freeman's Journal and Catholic Register.* "When he was announced to preach at St. Ignatius Church, San Francisco,...streams of people [were] turned away at the door. Hundreds of converts are to his credit, and a whole generation of the faithful among whom he labored will feel that, in his death, a household friend has been lost."

■ *(Courtesy of the Midwest Jesuit Archives)*

The Missouri Jesuits' attention was turning from western missions to urban education in the 1850s. As treasurer, De Smet helped inaugurate ministries at St. Gall's Parish, Milwaukee, and Holy Family Parish, Chicago. But he jumped at a chance to go west in 1858 to scout for a mission among the Blackfeet, this time as an army chaplain. He left the army to winter with the Cœur d'Alènes, who anticipated "a dark and somber future."

Hunger for land, gold, profits, and military and political advantage drove United States policies. Railroads began to cut the plains. Dependence on military contracts induced Union Pacific Railroad employees to instigate warfare, spreading false rumors of "Indian attacks."

Already an activist, De Smet voiced truth and spoke for justice. As an agent of the Indian Office in the 1860s, he carried to Washington, even to President Lincoln, complaints of "numerous injustices and misdeeds...of agents of the Government, [who]...deceived the Indians with impunity in the sale of their holdings of land...open theft." He stopped representing the government lest "the bearer of the word of the Great Spirit...[should] appear in their midst as the bearer of the word of the Big Chief of the Big Knives in Washington...now their greatest and bitterest enemy."

It is hard to reconcile De Smet the advocate of Native Americans with De Smet the friend of fur-company magnates and military and government officials. Warm, congenial, he may have loved individuals without challenging them. Perhaps he worked within the assumption that the westward Euro-American migration was an unstoppable force.

Patrick Healy (1834 -1910)

■ *Patrick Healy around 1873 (Photo by Julius Ulke, courtesy of Georgetown University Archives)*

Transforming Georgetown College (Washington, DC, USA) from a secondary and collegiate school into a university, Patrick Healy led Jesuit education into the modern era. He combined academic ideals and institutional vision.

As prefect of studies, Healy gave academics undisputed priority in college life. This brilliant, European-trained philosophy professor expanded the place of physical sciences in the curriculum, while raising standards in the classics and including more English literature. Becoming president at thirty-five, he consolidated the allied medical and law schools within Georgetown.

Healy understood the developmental nature of educational issues and unrelentingly drove his colleagues as well as himself in the pursuit of his goals. He exhausted himself, overseeing the building of a major facility (named the Healy Building after his tenure). The project was a leap of faith in Georgetown's future. Fundraising to make it a reality took President Healy across the country.

His health suffered—headaches and weak spells, perhaps undiagnosed epilepsy. A serious fall in 1882 precipitated his resignation. Limited parish ministry opened up, first in the diocese of his brother, Bishop James Healy. The nine Healy sisters and brothers, outstanding on different life paths, remained extraordinarily close, bound by their unusual history. Their parents Michael and Mary Eliza Healy, an Irish immigrant father and African-American slave mother, had defied the racial code in Georgia by establishing a home and family as a couple.

Sent north to be educated, Patrick and his siblings were baptized while the brothers studied at Holy Cross in Worcester, Massachusetts. Ten-year-old Patrick described his baptism as the beginning of "a new and more perfect life." More generous, more: *magis*.

The "Second Founder of Georgetown" died in 1910. He left an historic legacy to the Society, the Church, and American higher education.

With a nineteenth-century perspective, he addressed particular wrongs without fully grasping the systemic corruption.

De Smet had lost hope for peace and justice. He recognized that armed resistance would bring "total destruction and ruin" to the people he loved. His new mission, a sad one, was counseling survival instead of combat. His last hope was for a territory, limited but safe, where Native Americans might lead an agricultural life accommodated to the white invasion.

This was his message for the Sioux Peace Ride of 1868. With Eagle Woman and Charles Galpin and Chief Running Antelope, De Smet rode to the camp of Sitting Bull, carrying a banner of Mary as a sign of peace. Trusting the Blackrobe, tribal representatives signed a treaty at Fort Rice. The peace did not last on either side.

By 1870 government policy assigned many Catholic missions to Protestant pastors, despite De Smet's protests. Back in St. Louis after a last European trip, he was confined by Bright's Disease. Facing a new frontier, he asked for the last rites, "full of courage and hope," according to Bishop Patrick Ryan. On May 23, 1873, he died.

Memorials in St. Louis; Salt Lake City; De Smet, South Dakota; and Dendermonde, Belgium, commemorate him whom the Sioux called Watankanga Waokia, "The Man Who Shows His Love for the Great Spirit."

Gerard Manley Hopkins (1844-1889)

"Jesuit poet" is how the world remembers Gerard Manley Hopkins, placing his "Jesuitness" as an adjective. The man himself, however, chose to be a Jesuit first and foremost. Never defined by others' expectations, Hopkins lived from deep inside, with intense yearning, sensitivity and commitment. His single-minded and unyielding nature was tempered by introspection and struggle—the "war within."

Alice and Manley Hopkins of Essex, England, nourished the inner life through painting, music and poetry. Young Gerard, their eldest, developed an eye for visual detail, an ear for rhythm, a relish for words—delight in beauty.

At Highgate School Gerard excelled as a scholar but got into trouble by following his own judgments rather than Headmaster Dyne's regulations. Once he abstained from drinking any liquids for a week to prove a point. Later he frankly remarked, "I had no love for my school days."

Winning a competitive scholarship took him to Balliol College of Oxford University at nineteen. In its intellectual and social climate, Hopkins made life-long friendships. Anglicans at Balliol felt the influence of the Oxford Movement, a quest for religious authenticity that had led some

Gerard Manley Hopkins in 1880 (Used by permission of the Society of Jesus [British Province])

of their predecessors to Roman Catholicism. What did it mean that the Church is "one, holy, Catholic and apostolic"? Hopkins anguished, probed, prayed, talked with friends, consulted a Benedictine monk. Finally, in July 1866, he wrote in his journal, "I saw clearly."

He sought advice from Cardinal John Henry Newman, whose own quest had begun the Oxford Movement. Then he wrote to his parents, breaking the news of his conversion to Catholicism. "Their answers are terrible. I cannot read them twice." They begged their son to reconsider, to postpone

Jesuit formation

Candidacy

Novitiate: spiritual preparation for Jesuit life through experiences of prayer (including 30 days of the Spiritual Exercises) and experiences of ministry (such as teaching religion, serving the poor); 2 years

First vows: poverty, chastity and obedience and a promise to enter the Society

First Studies: study of philosophy and theology; 3 years

Regency: period of ministry with Jesuit and lay colleagues; 2-3 years

Theologate: study of theology; 3-4 years
- ordination (candidates for priesthood)

Ministry or further studies; 3-5 years

Tertianship, "School of the heart": includes 30 days of the Spiritual Exercises, a refresher course about the Society's history and spirit, and apostolic experience; up to 1 year

Final vows: poverty, chastity, obedience and availability to serve the greatest needs of the Church as assessed by the Pope

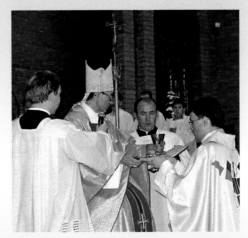

Bishop Joseph Werth, S.J., ordains his brother Klemens in 2002 at the Transfiguration Cathedral of Novosibirsk. Klemens was the first Russian Jesuit ordained to the priesthood in Russia after an Independent Region of the Society was established in 1992 (including Kazakhstan, Kyrgyzstan, Ukraine and Belarus). Joseph was elected president of the Russian Catholic Bishops' Conference in 2004/5. (Photo courtesy of Company *magazine.)*

a step which would close so many doors to his future. There was no stopping him. The convert wrote to his father, "I cannot fight against God Who calls me to His Church." Nor could he live without the sacraments, especially the Eucharist, "the life of the soul." Newman received Hopkins into the Church on October 21, 1866. Hopkins graduated with high honors in 1867, at the top of his class in Classics and "Greats" and finally at peace with his family.

What did God want him to do next? He taught briefly, then made a retreat in spring 1868. His journal notes, "May 5. Cold. Resolved to be a religious.... May 7. Warm. Misty morning; then beautiful turquoise sky. Home, after having decided to be a priest and religious but still doubtful between St. Benedict and St. Ignatius." In September he entered the Jesuit novitiate in Roehampton.

Studies took him to Stonyhurst after his first vows in 1870, then to Wales. The aspiring painter had laid aside his brush. The aspiring poet had burned his poems. Yet this period was an apprenticeship both for Jesuit life and for poetry.

His vivid journals and letters; study of the Welsh language; deepening, Christ-centered spirituality—all refined the ore.

Poetry burst forth in "The Wreck of the *Deutschland,*" after his rector had expressed a wish for verses about a shipwreck that had taken 157 lives on December 7, 1875, including those of five Franciscan sisters. Commemorating them, Hopkins interweaves his own spiritual journey, as

"There lives the dearest freshness deep down things...." ("*God's Grandeur." Photo by Lawrence Durkin*)

he "fled with a fling of the heart to the heart of the Host." Plunging into issues of suffering and death, he looks to Christ: "Let him easter in us, be a dayspring to the dimness of us, be a crimson-crested east."

More poems poured out. Intensely he focused on what he called the "inscape" of a thing, its distinctly individual reality, held in being by an energy he called "instress." "There lives the dearest freshness deep down things," he sang in "God's Grandeur." His nature poetry penetrates to "that being indoors each one dwells," its divine depth.

Originality in form, rhythm and vocabulary, even to coining words—innovation—was natural for Hopkins. "The effect of studying masterpieces is to make me admire and do otherwise." He replied to the criticism by his old friend Robert Bridges that some poems were obscure, acknowledging that readers would need to exert themselves to understand. The few times he submitted works for publication, they were turned down. He wished that they would "sometime...become known but...without my forcing."

And so they were, after his death, on the initiative of Bridges.

The Jesuit threw himself into ministry. Poems such as "The Bugler's First Communion," "At the Wedding March" and "Felix Randal" offer glimpses of his brief parish work among people he came to love. More often, he taught. In 1884, he was appointed to the Chair of Classics at University College, Dublin. Far from friends and family, he was lonely. He doubted his ability and overworked with a perfectionist's compulsion. "Work, worry and languishment of body and soul" brought on the depression that screams through his "terrible sonnets," from "that coffin of weakness and dejection in which I live." He cried, "Comforter, where, where is your comforting?"

At last the darkness lifted; a few years of relative peace followed. His health, always weak, remained fragile. When typhoid fever and peritonitis struck him down at 44, he wrote to his mother, "At many such a time I have been in a sort of extremity of mind, now I am the placidest soul in the world." On June 8, 1889, Gerard Manley Hopkins received his last Communion. He whispered, "I am so happy, so happy." They were his final words.

In 1975, England honored the memory of Gerard Manley Hopkins with a plaque in the Poets' Corner of Westminster Abbey.

Jacques Berthieu (1838-1896)

A good shepherd, Jacques Berthieu was one of many pastors who have shared the lives of their flock and have not fled when the wolf threatened.

Madagascar was struggling against British and French control. In 1883 France responded with war. Queen Ranavalona III resisted in 1894. French forces occupied the capital Antananarivo in September 1895 and declared Madagascar a colony in 1896. Equating Christianity with western colonialism, the independence movement aimed to restore indigenous cults. All Christians were at risk, especially Europeans.

Commitment brought Jacques Berthieu to the threshold of heroism. Courage and self-sacrifice led him the rest of the way—to martyrdom. No one would have expected the industrious French peasant to be a hero in a foreign land, certainly not himself.

Jacques' life started in the small world of a village in France's Massif Central. His father, a respected farmer, and his gentle, pious mother reared their seven children to be concerned about others. Jacques studied hard in school, just a few minutes' walk from home.

Hearing a call to priesthood early, he went to the seminary at sixteen. After ordination in 1863, he was assigned to a parish close to his widowed mother and other relatives. Patient and flexible, Jacques endured a hostile pastor; the next pastor was more compatible.

Dutiful Father Berthieu earned the respect of the parishioners and of the diocesan authorities of Saint-Flour. Soon he would be a pastor. All was going well.

Martyrs of the Boxer Rebellion (d. 1900)

China struggled between Western modernity and Eastern tradition, as the Boxer Rebellion shook its fist at "foreign devils."

In the region of Zhi-li (now Hopeh), sixty Jesuits served a Catholic community of 50,000, plus catechumens. Four of the sixty accepted the seal of martyrdom upon their missionary vocations; 30,000 lay Catholics were martyred.

June 18 and 19, 1900: Fathers Remi Isoré and Modeste Andlauer spent two days besieged in Wuyi. When the Boxers broke down the mission gate, they found the two Jesuits kneeling in the chapel. Parishioners retrieved their bodies, each pierced by a spear.

July 14 to 20, 1900: Father Leon-Ignace Mangin had fortified the mission of Zhujiahe to protect 3000 Catholic refugees from the Boxers. Battle raged for several days. In midnight darkness, some Christians escaped. Mangin and Father Paul Denn refused the opportunity, preferring to stay with their community.

On July 20 the besiegers mounted scaling towers. Further defense was futile, and over 1000, mostly women and children, gathered in the church.

Over roaring gunfire, Denn intoned, "I confess to Almighty God, to you, my brothers and sisters...." and the Act of Contrition. Mangin gave general absolution and promised, "Just a few minutes more and we shall all be in heaven."

The attackers burst in and offered to spare anyone who would forsake the faith. Only a few fled. As shooting began, a heroic woman climbed on the Communion rail, trying to protect Mangin. In the rain of bullets, she fell, then he. A catechist tried to raise him, but the Jesuit turned to die facing the crucifix. When Denn was shot, he struggled to kneel at Mangin's side. Then the roof caught fire. Men leaped from the windows, only to be shot as they emerged.

A community of 1370—priests and laity, adults and babies—died faithful to Christ, together.

Saints Remi, Modest, Leon-Ignace and Paul are celebrated on February 4, with other Jesuit martyrs. Fifty-two lay martyrs have also been canonized.

But was it? What was fermenting in the heart of this man, who seemed so well settled? At 35, wider horizons began to open up inside him. A new dimension of his vocation asserted itself: to be a Jesuit. On October 31, 1873, he entered the Society's novitiate in Pau. Suddenly he was a novice, among much younger men. Once again a student, he brushed up on his theology among the ninety other scholastics at Vals-près-le-Puy from 1874 to 1875.

There Berthieu's open heart was set afire by the Heart of Christ. He described a visiting preacher as speaking about "the theology of the Heart of Jesus...with a mastery, abundance and liveliness of expression and action that enlightened the mind and reached the heart." Missionary fervor was stirring the scholasticate. A Syrian student's account of his father's martyrdom impressed Berthieu deeply. He volunteered and was accepted, as he wrote, "to be apostle of the Malagasies."

Near Christmas 1875, he was one of four Jesuits arriving on the tiny island of Sainte-Marie off Madagascar, Berthieu's mission field for almost six years. Then came the first of the expulsions that would punctuate his ministry. Colonial authorities were applying the 1880 decree expelling religious from French soil. Berthieu's diary recounts the heart-rending separation from the "poor little people" he loved.

His next assignment took him to the Betsileos people of Ambohiminandroso, on Madagascar's central plateau. In 1883 he was expelled to northern territories under French control, where he served as military chaplain and missionary.

An interlude of peace opened in 1886. Berthieu moved to Ambositra, where lay leader Benedict Rakotonavalona and the priest-less Christian community had kept the faith. They royally welcomed their new pastor. City authorities were not so welcoming, however. Berthieu stood solidly with his parishioners, appearing with them

in court when they suffered injustices. They called him "a father who did not abandon his children." Besides the city and several schools, he served fifteen mission stations.

Almost six years later, the Jesuit was transferred. Once again, he suffered "heart-pangs" at the separation. Once again he embraced a new community of faith, in Andrainarivo.

Tension. Displacement. Finally, violence.

Berthieu learned that he was the main target of Rabozaka, leader of the Menalamba, a revolutionary movement. "Kill all Christians! Kill all whites! Most of all, kill Berthieu!"

When French authorities displaced his people, Berthieu accompanied them. They slept in open-air camps while the Menalamba sacked and burned their homes. He defended his flock from the brutal troops of Colonel Combes, who were infamous for rape and abuse of children. Marcello Rainimanantoamina wrote to the bishop, "without him we would be like chicks who have lost their mama."

The loss would come soon. Berthieu wrote to his family, "We await...the 'end that will never end.'"

On June 7, 1896, the 2000 refugees were sent south, carrying what few belongings they could manage. Berthieu gave his horse to a man who could not walk. The old and sick, the families with children lagged behind. The pastor was with them when Menalamba forces descended upon the stragglers. The desperate people managed to reach a friendly Protestant village and protection for a night.

June 8 began with Mass. Suddenly Menalamba raiders rushed through the village gates, demanding the priest and threatening destruction. At last a young man handed Berthieu over.

The story of that day's long forced march could be a catalogue of blows, mockery and outrage. Perhaps it is better to tell of the prisoner's gentle spirit, of his calling his torturers "my sons."

Passing the mission of Ambohitsara, he gave a crucifix to a neophyte and urged him to pray and to seek Baptism. "My lad," he said, "we won't see each other again, but remember today." Stripped to his underwear, shivering in the cold rain, the Jesuit maintained a calm dignity.

As night fell, his captors decided to make an end of him. The priest knelt. He extended his arms in the form of the cross. "Sacred Heart of Jesus, have mercy on me! Holy Mary, pray for me!" He faced the gunners. They shot and missed. He made the sign of the cross.

The captain had second thoughts and offered the condemned man a reprieve: "Renounce your wicked religion; ...we'll make you our counselor and not kill you."

"I prefer to die" were his last words.

Five shots rang out. Then the captain struck a final blow. They threw Berthieu's body into a crocodile-infested river, from which it was never recovered.

In 1965, Jacques Berthieu became the first person of Madagascar to be beatified. He is venerated on June 8 in France, on February 4 elsewhere.

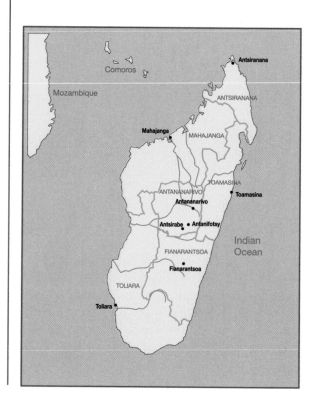

Chapter VI

The Crucible
of Transformation

*"What is it to be a companion of Jesus today?
It is to engage, under the standard of the Cross,
in the crucial struggle of our times:
the struggle for faith and that struggle
for justice which it includes."
(32nd General Congregation)*

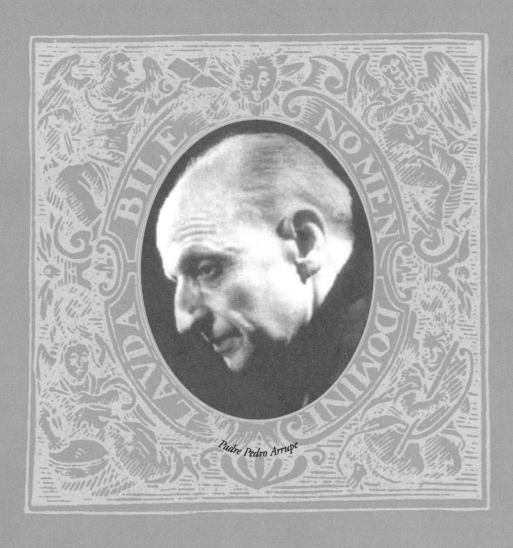

Padre Pedro Arrupe

The Crucible
of Transformation

The twentieth-century Society continued heroic ministries in the jaws of war and under threat from Nazism and Communism. Jesuits could be justly proud of their dedicated labors in universities, schools and parishes, in laboratories and missions, in retreat centers and street ministries and communications. They faced each major threat to faith. By 1965 the Society had over 36,000 members.

Great Jesuit thinkers had been exploring how to speak of faith in a world scarred by war and stimulated by science. They studied Scripture with the new tools offered by linguistics and archaeology. They reflected on the Gospel in the context of oppression. Jesuits contributed to the Second Vatican Council both in person and through their writings.

The 31st General Congregation (1965-1966) opened during the Council and held a second session to respond to its challenge, beginning the process of renewal and adaptation grounded in the Society's founding spirit and mission. After more than a century of semi-monastic practices, the assembly reclaimed the early Jesuits' missionary style of life.

The 32nd General Congregation (1974-1975) undertook a more communal transformation. It grounded Jesuit identity in a mission of faith and justice and in "a communion of life and work and sacrifice." The congregation urged a meaningful practice of poverty. Decree 4, "The Service of Faith and the Promotion of Justice," critiqued unjust systems and committed Jesuits to act for justice. The results appeared in solidarity with peasants, in educational ministries among the urban underclass, in research and teaching toward systemic justice. Slurs and labels of "subversive" highlighted the tension surrounding these developments, from inside and outside the Society. Yet creative ministries multiplied.

The Society ended the century with about 22,000 men. In Africa and Asia, membership had multiplied, while it had slumped in Europe and North America. In accord with the practice of the Founders, collaboration was transforming almost all Jesuit ministries in ever-expanding circles of lay men and women.

A late-20th-century interpretation of St. Ignatius by Manuel Cusachs now inhabits a niche in the façade of Antonio Gaudí's Temple of the Holy Family *in Barcelona. The statue's inscription quotes the Contemplation to Attain Divine Love in the Spiritual Exercises: "En tot servir y estimar" (In all things to serve and to love). (Photo montage, Yearbook S.J. 2004, courtesy of the Society of Jesus Office of Press and Information)*

Century of Conflict, Century of Renewal

Twentieth-century consciousness expanded from national to global. The century closed with a millennial experience shared literally around the world. Cell phones, televisions and computers linked millions, of every continent, on New Year's Day 2000.

■ *Cardinal Augustin Bea, S.J., worked closely with Pope John XXIII, beginning the Church's Secretariat for Ecumenism and fostering an open spirit in the Second Vatican Council. Dedicated to Christian unity, Bea also encouraged dialogue with other religions. (Courtesy of Society of Jesus Office of Press and Information)*

Political and social ferment reshaped boundaries. European conflicts ignited World War I, but this "war to end all wars" drew in European colonies and the Western Hemisphere. World War II provided the worst of humanity's inhumanity: the Jewish Holocaust in Europe and the atomic bombing of Japan by the United States. India and many other Asian and African peoples threw off colonial control.

In the century's second half, the Cold War polarized the world around American capitalist and Soviet communist superpowers. As the latter crumbled, regional conflicts multiplied. Vast divisions between wealthy and impoverished peoples became more visible as wars, famine, poverty and persecution created millions of refugees.

Popular movements strove to liberate the oppressed: rights for indigenous peoples, land-reform, respect for sexual minorities.... Women sought equality with men in every sphere. Communications media flashed awareness everywhere. Computers transformed human endeavors and consciousness itself.

Communist governments often persecuted religion; Catholics responded as noble martyrs and as vigorous anti-Communist activists.

Opening the Church to fresh air, Pope John XXIII convoked the Second Vatican Council (1962-1965), bishops and observers from every land. With joy and hope and faith in the Holy Spirit, they called for renewal in liturgy, theology, social communications, ecumenism. They and subsequent bishops' conferences called the world to create peace and justice. The Council instructed religious orders to seek renewal in their original founding spirit.

By 2000, the powerful figure of Pope John Paul II was a beacon of faith for the nations and a re-centralizing force within the Church.

■ *In St. Peter's Basilica, the Second Vatican Council initiated the renewal called for by Pope John XXIII. (Photo by Lawrence Durkin)*

Heroic Witnesses

"Witness gives the ideal flesh and blood." – Pedro Arrupe

William Doyle (1873-1917)

A true companion of Jesus was William Doyle—loving and joyful, serving and suffering, leading others to God and giving up his life for his friends.

The youngest of seven in a comfortable family of Dalkey, near Dublin, Willie could have been a spoiled child. Quite the opposite, he loved to help, washing dishes for the cook and visiting poor neighbors. He used to take food to an elderly woman with a yen for tobacco, which he also managed to provide. He scrubbed her floors and washed her walls.

Sent to boarding school at eleven, Willie worked at his studies but excelled in sports and fun. He salvaged one escapade with more tobacco. Four friends had decided to roast and eat a duck. But where? Willie figured out how to slide down the coal chute into the furnace room. Just as the feast was ready, Jasper, the furnace-man, caught them by surprise. They were dead ducks, for sure! But Willie wheedled Jasper with promises of tobacco and saved the day.

Camaraderie and good humor made him everybody's favorite schoolmate.

Being a soldier was Willie's earliest dream. He begged his mother to make him a uniform and told her, after a trip to the barber, "Soldiers do not wear curls." By his teens, he was thinking of priesthood, which also demanded courage and self-sacrifice. Jesus would be his hero.

His older brother Charlie entered the Society and invited Willie to consider it. "Never!" Willie planned to be a diocesan priest. His mind seemed closed, but his heart must have been open. On Christmas Day 1890, his father found Willie alone at the piano and asked him about the future. A surprising answer tumbled out: he wanted to be a Jesuit. Having put his vocation into words, he turned to the keyboard and put into music the joy of accepting it.

Eagerly he entered the Tullabeg novitiate on March 31, 1891, running up the front steps three at a time.

Eagerness for complete self-giving grew into a desire for martyrdom, a desire that he wrote in his own blood. Yearning intensely to share the sufferings of Jesus, he undertook harsh physical penances. They were extreme expressions of a young man's courage and love.

■ *William Doyle, military chaplain (Reproduced courtesy of the Irish Province)*

Yet gentleness always flowed out to others. As a regent "Mr. Doyle" taught at Clongowes Wood. An excellent athlete, he enjoyed working with sports activities. After he had arbitrated one close cricket match, an angry loser called him a "damned cheat." How would Mr. Doyle respond? The boys waited. A few days later, the culprit apologized. Doyle smiled, giving him cookies and advice that the youngster was now ready to accept.

For philosophy studies Doyle was sent to Belgium, then to Stonyhurst, England, in 1899. An Irishman among the English, he expressed views on the Boer War that differed from his fellow-students' ideas. Yet he won their affection. "When an act of kindness was to be done," one later remembered, "Willie Doyle was there to do it."

Theology studies proved difficult. "You know I was never intended by Almighty God to keep my nose buried in books all day. Climbing up chimneys or walking on my head across the roof of a house is more in my line."

Doyle was ordained a priest on July 28, 1907. Soon he was assigned to the mission staff, traveling to parishes and schools for programs of spiritual renewal. His effectiveness as a preacher and a confessor resulted from his closeness to the Christ of whom he spoke, a loving intimacy that came through deep prayer.

He drew souls to God, like the prostitute whom he encountered on a street one night in Yarmouth, England. He paused in concern, saying, "My child, aren't you very late? Won't you go home? Don't hurt Jesus. He loves you."

Two years later an urgent telegram came from a London prison, where a convict on death row was asking for a nameless Irish Jesuit who had been in Yarmouth. It was the prostitute. Fanny Cranbush remembered his words and his gaze, "which seemed to go right through me." In her cell the young priest instructed and baptized Fannie, offered Mass and gave her Communion. Then he accompanied her to the scaffold. She whispered, "I am so happy! Jesus knows that I am sorry for having hurt him, and I know that Jesus loves me."

Doyle's final service would require his every gift of body, heart, mind and spirit, his every skill. He volunteered as a chaplain early in World War I. He was assigned to the 8th Royal Irish Fusiliers, 16th Division, sent into action in France in February 1916. Accompanying his "boys" in the trenches meant mud, rats, fleas, bone-chilling cold and immersion in death. In May a German shell exploded in his trench; "the two men who had been standing on my left hand...were stretched on the ground dead, though I think I had time to give them absolution and anoint them."

One dying lad opened his eyes, whispered "Ah, Fr. Doyle, Fr. Doyle," then embraced the priest, grateful that he had not been left to die alone and without the sacraments.

Doyle's bravery at the Somme won him the Military Cross.

His letters were mostly cheerful, not to cause worry at home. "Everyone loves [our Irish lads]— the French girls naturally.... It is quite amusing to hear them point out my dug-out... 'That's *our* priest,' with a special stress on the 'our.'"

Yet he also shared war's horror and pathos, such as this post-battle description: "Some lay as if they were sleeping quietly, others had died in agony...while the whole ground, every foot, was littered with heads or limbs, or pieces of torn human bodies. In the bottom of one hole lay a British and a German soldier, locked in a deadly embrace, neither had any weapon but they had fought on to the bitter end. Another couple seemed to have realised that the horrible struggle was none of their making, and that they were both children of the same God; they had died hand-in-hand."

His last letter to "Dearest Father" ended, "Heaps of love to every dear one."

His new battalion, 8th Royal Dublin Fusiliers, saw action at Langemarck on August 16, 1917. Although retreat was sounded, Chaplain Doyle would not leave the fallen. Under enemy fire he crawled out to a wounded man and dragged him toward safety. As Doyle tried to give the soldier a drink of water, a mortar shell blew them both into eternity.

A hasty battlefield grave received this hero's body. It has never been found.

Miguel Agustín Pro (1891-1927)

Anti-Catholic policies embedded in Mexico's 1857 Constitution escalated in the 1920s. Revolutionary forces turned on the Church, which had often allied itself with the wealthy classes. President Plutarco Elías Calles closed Catholic schools and attacked the clergy in 1924. Religious services were outlawed as of July 31, 1926. Priests were criminals, unless they agreed to the nationalization of churches.

However, the Church was also the peasant, the professional, the laborer. Political and even armed resistance were widespread. Public religious demonstrations and underground worship nourished faith. Thousands were executed, many crying, "¡Viva Cristo Rey!" (Long live Christ the King!)

Entering a room where Jesuits were debating the pros and cons of some topic, a young Mexican punster introduced himself, "You are contra, I am Pro."

Miguel Agustín Pro's story is both comedy and adventure, the tale of a clown who was a hero and a saint.

A mimic with a miner's vocabulary, a quick wit and a way with the guitar, Miguel was a natural entertainer. He picked up salty language by accompanying his father, a mining engineer, to the mines near Zacatecas. At fifteen, Miguel left school to work in his father's office. He spent his free time underground with the miners and would later sign letters "The Miner."

When his two older sisters entered religious life, he resented their loss from the family circle but was inspired by the Ignatian question, "Jesus Christ suffered all this for us; what do we do for him?" He entered the Society at El Llano in 1911 and made vows in 1913.

A year later the student Jesuits were hemmed in by revolutionary violence. Incognito, they escaped to the Society's novitiate in Los Gatos, California. Miguel's father was in hiding and his mother, with the younger children, was impoverished.

By 1920 he was in Spain, studying philosophy. As a regent he taught in Nicaragua, then returned to Europe for theology, first in Spain and then in Enghien, Belgium. There he was ordained in 1925. He got involved with the Young Catholic Workers. In ecstasy at Lourdes, he "felt profoundly... [Mary's] blessed presence."

Everywhere Miguel entertained his companions. He organized picnics, pantomimes and performances. He gave no clues of the digestive problems that caused him so much pain that three surgeries were eventually required. Nor did others witness his worry and homesickness or his anguish at the news of his beloved mother's death.

Returning to Mexico City (where his family had relocated) in July 1926, the priest would soon be an outlaw. It was a role he relished almost as much as being "of use to souls."

Clandestine Masses... Approaching a house where he was to celebrate, and finding two policemen on guard, he jotted the address in a notebook, turned his coat lapel to flash an imaginary badge and declared with official pomp, "Something fishy going on in here!" As he entered, the police gave "two magnificent military salutes" to the priest they had been sent to arrest.

The police raided during another Mass, only to find a cocky gentleman in a cap and a gray suit, smoking a cigarette in a long, elegant holder.

Underground retreats.... Chauffeurs and truck-drivers—"lads of gold"—listened in a fenced lot to a preacher dressed as a mechanic, "a cap well down over my forehead."

Secret confessions.... A reserve officer threatened to arrest him, until Pro pointed out that he would not then be able to hear the confession of the officer's mother.

Wild pursuits.... Leaping into a taxicab, the fugitive directed the driver to turn a corner, whereupon he leaped out and leaned so nonchalantly against a tree that the pursuing police car grazed his leg as it swept on after the cab.

Hairsbreadth escapes.... Racing around another corner into an alley, he saw a woman he knew, gave her a wink and took her arm. A moment later his pursuers rounded the same corner to find only a couple of strolling lovers.

Pro was begging and delivering food for impoverished families—lugging sacks of flour and once boarding a bus with six live chickens. He was training youth leaders. The League for the Defense of Religious Liberty broadcast his talks on radio until the government located and shut down the transmitter.

"Do you know...where I learned to love? It was in the Heart of Jesus."

The Pro family shared a commitment to religious liberty. Brothers Humberto and Roberto both served time in prison for anti-government activities. All became targets.

In September 1927, Father Pro "offered my life for the saving of Mexico, and this morning at Mass I felt it had been accepted."

The three Pro brothers were asleep when several officers threw open the door and placed them under arrest. Roberto wanted to make his confession, and Miguel kept the police waiting until he had conferred absolution on his godson.

They were charged with the attempted assassination of the powerful General Obregón. During five days in foul dungeons, Miguel encouraged his fellow prisoners and led them in prayer and laughter. There were no legal proceedings, only a smear campaign in the press.

At 10:20 a.m. on November 23, a prison guard called out, "Miguel Augustín Pro!" The prisoner emerged from his cell and was sent back for his jacket. He squeezed Roberto's hand. Then one of the arresting officers asked his pardon. Pro replied, "Not only do I forgive you, but I thank you." Having expected a trial, he was just now realizing what lay ahead.

In the courtyard nicknamed "garden of death," military officers and photographers stood in witness. Pro asked time for prayer and knelt with his hands crossed on his breast, slowly made the sign of the cross and kissed the crucifix he had

drawn from his pocket. In his other hand was his rosary.

Then he faced the squad, refusing to be blindfolded. "May God have mercy on you. May God bless you," he said to all. "Lord, you know that I am innocent." Opening his arms in the form of a cross, he added, "I forgive my enemies with all my heart."

The troops took aim. The martyr finished: *"Viva Cristo Rey!"*

Humberto's martyrdom followed immediately. Roberto was spared at the last moment. Outside the prison, their sister Ana María heard the shots. She claimed the bodies at the morgue. Old Señor Pro wiped the bloody faces of his sons and told his weeping daughter, "This is no cause for tears." The funeral of the Pro brothers was a triumphal procession, accompanied by thousands.

Miguel Agustín Pro was beatified in 1988. His feast is November 23.

■ *Pro kneels in prayer before his execution in the Garden of Death, between targets used for shooting practice. (Courtesy of the Society of Jesus Office of Press and Information)*

■ *Miguel Pro faces the firing squad with arms outstretched in the form of Christ's cross. (Courtesy of the Society of Jesus Office of Press and Information)*

Rupert Mayer (1876-1945)

Facing hostile fire was part of authentic pastoral ministry for Rupert Mayer, whether in the trenches or in the pulpit.

A military chaplain had to be in personal contact with the front-line troops, Father Mayer insisted. He had volunteered to serve young men who were facing death as German soldiers in World War I. He faced it with them. During one fire-fight, the stretcher-bearers took shelter and left their patient on the field. Chaplain Mayer shielded the wounded boy, encouraging him, "Don't be afraid! If shrapnel comes, it will hit me first."

His "example of fearlessness" won Mayer the Iron Cross, First Class, the army's highest decoration. Shattered by a shell, his left leg required amputation. He learned to walk with a prosthesis; a limp testified to his heroism.

The war had interrupted his pastoral work among Munich's transients. Thousands had been pouring into the city from rural villages, seeking work and housing. Mayer had been assigned in 1912 to help the diocese assist these homeless,

unemployed and often desperate people. He and the 5,600 volunteers he mobilized went from hovel to hovel. They guided newcomers to find work, navigate the city's complexities and connect with a parish. Personal contact was his watchword.

After the war, Mayer applied his organizational skills to spiritual renewal. He led a citywide mission in late 1919, engaging 3,600 lay volunteers. Under his influence the Sodality of Our Lady, a venerable Jesuit-inspired movement of lay spiritual development, tripled its membership to 8,000. Sodalists worked with their pastors for renewal at the parish level.

■ *Albert Hurtado, S.J. (1901-1952) and his family had been homeless. As a Jesuit, he initiated ministries for Chile's homeless people, Hogar de Cristo (Home of Christ). He was canonized in 2005. (Courtesy of Society of Jesus Office of Press and Information)*

Meanwhile, this powerful spiritual leader attended meetings of the new Communist Party to advocate a society based on faith and love. The National Socialists (Nazis) began to formulate a nationalistic future. Mayer attended their meetings too and challenged their anti-Semitic and totalitarian principles.

Mayer's popularity blocked the Nazis' interest in assassinating him. Hitler sent him greetings for the silver anniversary of his ordination in 1924; Mayer tore up the note and threw it into the wastebasket.

Hitler consolidated power and moved against Jews and against the Church. Hitler Youth attacked Catholic volunteers making a charity collection in 1935. Government propaganda sought to destroy Catholic schools and smeared clergy and religious orders.

Mayer challenged Nazi policies. He preached all over Germany, often twice or three times a day, even outdoors when the churches could not

■ *Rupert Mayer (Yearbook S.J. 2000, courtesy of Society of Jesus Office of Press and Information)*

accommodate the crowds. In 1937 the government forbade him to speak in public. His Provincial agreed that he might defy the order. The Gestapo arrested Mayer in June, to widespread public opposition.

After negotiations, a civilian court suspended his six-month sentence. Munich's Cardinal asked him to be quiet for a while, not to spark further persecution. With his Provincial's permission, Mayer preached on New Year's Day 1938, for the Society's titluar feast, the Name of Jesus. Re-arrest and four months of imprisonment followed immediately. The Cardinal directed him not to antagonize the Gestapo again. When he was released, Mayer ministered through personal contact in spiritual direction, confession and private meetings.

His next arrest came in October 1939, for "supporting movements hostile to the State." A member of the opposition party had sought Mayer's support, and although Mayer had not even welcomed the man, the conversation was held against him. Furthermore, the Gestapo wanted names of others in the opposition. Through repeated interrogations, Mayer would name no names.

The Oranienburg-Sachsenhousen concentration camp was the destination of a train that pulled out of Munich on December 22, carrying the Jesuit. Gestapo chief Heinrich Himmler had decided that he should be held without trial. After seven months, Mayer's deteriorating health alarmed the staff of the camp infirmary. What if the popular preacher, the decorated veteran amputee, should die in custody?

The solution was to confine him on August 7, 1940, at the Benedictine monastery of Ettal. No correspondence, visits allowed only from his nearest relatives, no contact with the outside world—"a death much worse than the real death I have faced so many times."

The Allied invasion of Germany brought liberation for the prisoner in May 1945. Once again he addressed the Sodality: "God has kept us alive and has a task for us to perform." His own task was interceding with the Occupation forces on behalf of fellow-countrymen who were unjustly treated.

He was exhausted. Celebrating Mass on November 1, he read the Gospel and spoke a few words, then "The Lord, the Lord, the Lord" before lapsing into unconsciousness. It was All Saints Day—Mayer's last day on earth.

Beatified in 1987, Rupert Mayer is commemorated on November 3.

Walter Ciszek (1904-1984)

■ *(Photo courtesy of the Walter Ciszek Prayer League)*

The Society answered Pope Paul VI's call for ministry to Catholics in the Soviet Union, cut off from their Church by Communist persecution. Incognito, Jesuits like Walter Ciszek volunteered to scout potential sites for the dangerous Russian Mission.

Who was this rugged logger at a lumber camp in the Ural Mountains? A Polish widower or an American Jesuit? Or a German—no, a Vatican—spy?

A spy, decided the Russian investigator in 1941. Walter Ciszek, alias Wladimir Martinovich Lipinski, was sentenced to fifteen years' hard labor. He had been a tough kid, a street-fighter, but grueling interrogations drove him close to suicide. Lonely, humiliated, he drew courage from his faith that God accompanied him. In Central Siberia's factories, docks and mines, he barely survived the brutal conditions. Yet he made friends and ministered to souls in need.

Released in 1956, Ciszek worked as a laboratory technician and an auto mechanic, always under surveillance. He was expelled from two cities for offering Mass and sacraments to spiritually famished people.

The Secret Police whisked him to Moscow in October 1963, without explanation. Only at the airport did he learn of an exchange of American and Russian prisoners. Ciszek was on his way home to America.

Servant of God Walter Ciszek spent the rest of his life speaking and writing as a witness of the faith that had sustained him.

Champions of Renewal

"We must take in the world entire, plumb its depths, before we can grasp its needs... and rise to their challenge." – Pedro Arrupe

Pierre Teilhard de Chardin (1881-1955)

"When men have harnessed the winds, the waves, the tides and gravity, they will harness for God the energies of love, and then for the second time in the history of the world, man will have discovered fire."
– Pierre Teilhard de Chardin, "The Evolution of Chastity"

World-famous paleontologist and mystic Pierre Teilhard de Chardin dug deep into love. Misunderstood and silenced, he experienced purification without becoming bitter. He was described as "an obedient but stubborn son of the Church."

His father introduced Pierre ("rock") to rocks and plants; the boy fell in love with the world. The "spark" that would "light up and fire my child's soul" he attributed to his mother.

Pierre was the fourth of eleven children, reared in Auvergne, France, within view of extinct volcanoes and wide plains. His family's piety and a Jesuit education fostered the vocation that led him to enter the Society in 1899. Shortly after he made

vows, anti-clerical legislation forced the French scholasticate's removal to the Isle of Jersey in 1902.

Three years of teaching science in Cairo introduced the young man to fascinating new terrain. He was discovering "the divine at the heart of a glowing universe." Ordained in 1911, he continued his scientific study and came to understand his vocation as a scientist and the "sacred duty of research," exploring reality.

Then came World War I. Father Teilhard declined a chaplaincy commission to serve as a stretcher-bearer on the front lines—"I can do more good there"—in France and Morocco. His citation for the Chevalier of the Legion of Honor speaks of his devotion to the foot soldiers, "whose dangers and hardships he constantly shared."

With a doctorate in paleontology from the Sorbonne, he taught and excavated. In geological strata and fossils, Teilhard probed earth's evolution. He found in it a process of growing consciousness and unification, driven by divine energy toward a goal, an "Omega Point": the

■ *The Chou-Hou-Tien team discovered the "Peking Man" (Sinanthropus) in 1929 (left to right): Pei Wenzhong, Dr. C. C. Young, Heng-Sheng Wang, Kung-Mu Wang, Pierre Teilhard de Chardin, Davidson Black and George Barbour. (Photo by permission of the Fondation Teilhard de Chardin)*

Cosmic Christ described in St. Paul's Epistle to the Colossians. Teilhard respected the distinct authenticity of both science and faith; he honored an organic relationship between them. His ideas were exciting. Students circulated notes on his lectures.

Wary of Modernism and of evolutionary ideas, some fellow-Jesuits worked against him, especially in Rome. Teilhard challenged literal readings of the Bible, challenged the idea that reality is divided into matter and spirit. Father General Ledochowski told him not to publish his philosophical or religious ideas. He should confine himself to science. In China—in exile.

Pierre Teilhard de Chardin (Yearbook S.J. 2000, courtesy of Society of Jesus Office of Press and Information)

Jesuits at the Second Vatican Council (1962-1965)

Behind the scenes at the Second Vatican Council, Jesuit experts contributed. Four played crucial roles, which Karl Rahner modestly described as "a bit mythologized."

Cardinal Augustine Bea (1881-1968) initiated the Secretariat for Christian Unity, which opened cordial communications with other Christians. He labored over the Decree on Ecumenism, laying foundations for the ecumenical movement. Bea also worked to heal relationships with the Jewish people and members of other religions.

Henri de Lubac (1896-1991) spent the 1950s in banishment for reasons that were never made clear to him by the Society. Removed from his teaching position in Lyon, he lived alone and was required to submit all his writings to Roman censors. Pope John XXIII appointed him as a consultor to the Theological Preparatory Commission. De Lubac's work on the sources of revelation fed into the decrees on Divine Revelation and on the Church in the Modern World.

New York Jesuit John Courtney Murray (1904-1967) suffered censorship when certain American partisans campaigned at the Vatican against his defense of the separation of Church and state. Nonetheless, American bishops relied on Murray as anti-Catholic propaganda emerged against John Kennedy's campaign for President. Cardinal Francis Spellman took him to the Council's second session as advisor. Murray's ideas infused the Declaration on Religious Freedom.

Karl Rahner (1904-1984) too incurred Vatican limitations on his publications. Cardinal Franz König involved him in the Council as theological expert. His influence appears in many Council declarations.

Henri de Lubac (left) and John Courtney Murray are vested for Mass on November 18, 1965, during the Second Vatican Council's final session. Pope Paul VI invited them and other theologians who had previously been silenced or under a cloud to concelebrate with him at this public event. (Courtesy of the New York Province Archives)

Karl Rahner (1904-1984)

Perhaps the greatest theologian of the twentieth century, Karl Rahner saw himself first as a human being who had experienced God, then as a Christian in love with Jesus Christ, then as a spiritual disciple of Ignatius Loyola and a priest of the Church. Finally, as a theologian, he put the fruits of thought and prayer at the service of pastoral needs.

And in very complex sentences!

Rahner's classical theological training led him to a professorship in Innsbruck, Austria, interrupted by World War II. Pastoral work during and after the war heightened his concern for individuals. He has been called "an everyday mystic." Prayer nourished his theology and preaching and made of him a teacher of prayer. His focus on Christ is in the spirit of the Contemplation to Attain Divine Love. Rahner credited Ignatius as the primary influence on his work.

As university professor (Innsbruck, Munich, Münster), expert at the Second Vatican Council, lecturer and author of 4000 titles, Rahner brought fresh insight to nearly all areas of theology.

Rahner called the 1980s the "wintry season" of retreat from the Council's spirit, while retaining hope that "the charismatic element is still very much alive" in the Church.

His assignment in 1926 was to the French Paleontological Mission, excavating fossil remains in the Mongolian steppes. Teilhard endeared himself to Chinese scientists because he cooperated with them and did not seek to remove their discoveries to Europe. When Pei Wenzhong unearthed a skull at Chou-Hou-Tien in 1929, Teilhard determined its age as about 500,000 years. His name will always be associated with this "Peking Man" *(Sinanthropus),* the oldest example of truly human beings who had evolved to the use of tools and fire.

The scientist cannot be separated from the philosopher/theologian, whose lofty ideas were deeply rooted in human experience. "God...is waiting for us...in our action, in our work of the moment. He is in some sort at the tip of my pen, my spade, my brush, my needle—of my heart and of my thought": humanity cooperating in Creation itself.

The philosopher was also a mystic and a poet. In the vast Ordos Desert, Teilhard completed his "Mass on [the altar of] the World," his prayer to "Glorious Lord Christ: the divine influence secretly diffused and active in the depths of matter, and the dazzling center...to whom my being cried out with a desire as vast as the universe, 'In truth you are my Lord and my God.'"

What of the man?

Teilhard's students and colleagues warmed to his kindly personal interest, as respectful to a teenager as to a diplomat. The Chinese named him "De Ri jin," loosely translated "Father Daybreak Virtue." He loved laughter, jokes and cartoons.

Teilhard needed dialogue, both to develop his ideas and to learn from others; he made friends around the world. Among his warmest friendships was with Lucile Swan, an American sculptor whom he first knew in Peiping (Beijing). They took tea together almost daily between 1929 and 1932 and maintained a devoted correspondence punctuated by visits until his death. Their letters reveal how Lucile challenged his commitment to chastity, while he insisted that he "belong[ed] to Something Else." Teilhard affirmed the noble role of sexual attraction to bodily union, but he asserted an alternative: a convergence of spirit.

The constraints on his work and restricted quarters during World War II sometimes reduced Teilhard to tears. When he returned to France in 1946, his ideas were being widely circulated by others. Fellow Jesuits urged publication. Father General Janssens, though, echoed his predecessor's prohibition. Friends urged Teilhard to leave the Society, but he wrote to Janssens, "You can count on me unreservedly to work for the Kingdom of God,...the one goal to which science leads me."

His sufferings included a heart attack, which taught him obedience to the diminishments of his own body. "O God, grant that I may understand that it is You who are painfully parting the fibres of my being in order to penetrate to the very marrow of my substance and bear me away within Yourself."

Europe had no place for him. The New York-based Wenner Gren Foundation for Anthropological Research invited him to America in 1951. It was a second exile.

On Easter Sunday 1955 Teilhard was visiting friends when he fell. After a moment he opened his eyes and said, "What's happened—where am I?" and "This time, I feel it's terrible." Then were his words fulfilled: "...him the earth will lift up, like a mother, in the immensity of her arms, and will enable him to contemplate the face of God."

Published after his death, Teilhard's writings found enthusiastic acceptance: The Phenomenon of Man, The Divine Milieu, *"The Mass on the World,"* The Future of Man, The Hymn of the Universe, *and others.*

Pedro Arrupe (1907-1991)

If a man counts his thirty-five days of solitary confinement as "the most instructive month of my entire life," he must have deep interior resources. If at its end he thanks his interrogator, he must have a great heart. Such a man was Pedro Arrupe, twenty-seventh successor of Ignatius Loyola, and a Basque.

One Basque had founded the Society, some said, and the second was destroying it. Others would call Arrupe "the third founder." Arrupe saw his mission in the late twentieth century not as imitating Ignatius the General but as applying the inspiration of Ignatius the Founder.

In Bilbao, close to Spain's northern Atlantic coast, four daughters were born to Marcelino and Dolores Arrupe, then a son, Pedro. Among the earliest memories of tiny "Perico" was accompanying his father in the Sacred Heart procession, conscious even then of God's love appearing in Jesus. Decades later, only one image hung in his office in Japan, the Chinese ideograph for the word "heart." The child's heart was wounded at ten by the death of his mother. Don Marcelino assured him that Mary would be his "Mother in heaven."

Guided and tutored by his sisters, Pedro did well in school and set his sights on a career in medicine, studying first at Valladolid and then in

■ *Pedro Arrupe (Courtesy of the Institute of Jesuit Sources)*

Pedro Arrupe's inspiration led to the creation of this shrine to the martyrs of Nagasaki. (Courtesy of the 26 Martyrs Shrine, Nagasaki, Japan)

Madrid. He relished dormitory life. The seventh-floor residents declared their independence of the dining hall and learned to cook, with much laughter and an occasional rescue by a student's mother. They went to bars and operas together and helped each other study. Many shared a commitment of faith and service in the St. Vincent de Paul Society. This volunteer work opened Pedro's eyes to a different world, Madrid's slums. The compassion awakened there would never leave him.

In Quito, Ecuador, Arrupe exchanges services with a shoeshine boy. (Photo courtesy of Company *magazine)*

Pedro regularly took top honors. Professor Juan Negrin, the Dean, foresaw in him one of Spain's "best future doctors."

In 1926, his last year at Madrid, came a death and a birth. Don Marcelino suffered partial paralysis and died with his children at his bedside. After that great loss, Pedro and his sisters traveled to Lourdes. "There was born my vocation.... at the feet of the Virgin Mary." He stayed three months observing the medical board, composed of atheists, who investigated supposed cures. Three were verified during his time there. "I had been the eyewitness of a true miracle. A miracle performed by...that same Jesus who had cured during his lifetime so many paralytics and sick people."

Pedro entered the Society in January 1927. An intimate spiritual experience, indescribable, called him to be a missionary in Japan, but Father General did not at once accept his application. When Spain expelled the Jesuits in 1932, Pedro continued his studies in Holland and was ordained there in 1936. Further studies, followed by tertianship, took him to the United States. The young Father Arrupe was becoming an international expert on medical ethics.

Ten years after his first request, in 1938 Arrupe was sent to a Japan that was on the brink of war with China and then with the United States. His first assignment was as a parish priest in Yamaguchi. Despite his month-long imprisonment (supposedly as a Western spy), Japan became the

Pedro Arrupe (Courtesy of Society of Jesus Office of Press and Information)

missionary's second homeland in his twenty-seven years there.

Understanding and entering into Japanese thought and culture were essential, the Jesuits believed. Arrupe described this "inculturation" as "the incarnation of the Christian life and message in a concrete cultural setting...." He learned Zen. Appointed master of novices in 1942, Arrupe recognized that he could not instruct young Japanese Jesuits in a European mode.

Then came the Americans' atomic bomb. By 8:10 a.m. on August 6, 1945, Arrupe had finished his Mass at the Nagatsuka novitiate. Even there, four miles from the epicenter in Hiroshima, Arrupe was blown to the floor. The Nagatsuka Jesuits found their injured brethren from the city

parish and managed to carry them to the novitiate.

The novitiate chapel became a field hospital, and Arrupe the emergency physician. Novices nursed the wounded. Sheets and underwear provided material for bandages. On August 7 Arrupe offered Mass amid the sufferers lying on the chapel floor. He spread his arms—"The Lord be with you"—and felt paralyzed. "They were all looking at me, eyes full of agony and despair." None were Christians. Six months later, when all patients had been able to leave (only two died), many had been baptized as a result of their encounter with Christ's love in the Jesuits.

Arrupe's postwar mission was to bear witness around the world about the horror of the bomb and to collect funds for Japan's recovery. (Besides Spanish and Latin, he spoke English, French, German, Japanese and Italian.)

As Vice-Provincial (1954) and then Provincial (1958) of Japan, Arrupe led men from thirty-some countries, because Japan was a mission of the entire Society. "It was a small universe," he said, "where we were receiving echoes from every-where." He brought his global vision to the 31st General Congregation in 1965. The assembled fathers elected him General. In that capacity he attended the last session of the Second Vatican Council.

The new Father General wanted to learn. The first General to travel widely, he visited every province, meeting his brothers, listening to them

Pope Paul VI and Father General Arrupe are pictured here in 1965. (Courtesy of Society of Jesus Office of Press and Information)

Padre Arrupe (right) and the newly elected Father General Peter-Hans Kolvenbach greet one another at the 33rd General Congregation, on September 13, 1983. (Courtesy of Society of Jesus Office of Press and Information)

attentively. He spoke with a sincerity that reached from deep in his heart to deep in theirs: "For me, Christ is everything." Arrupe trusted youth, trusted young Jesuits. He looked at the contemporary world with hope and had the courage to take risks. He learned from his mistakes and could laugh at himself.

The Second Vatican Council opened up heady days of experimentation throughout the Church, but also a time of uncertainty and of hemorrhage from religious orders. Not all Jesuits welcomed the results of the Council or the fresh approaches that the new General encouraged or allowed. Some experiments failed. Was he destroying the Society?

A group in Spain, calling themselves "the faithful Jesuits," wanted to separate from their province and maintain traditional ways. They enlisted support from Spain's bishops, bypassed the General and reached the ear of Pope Paul VI. Arrupe approached the Pope, who affirmed that he would not interfere. But the polarization in the Society remained. It was painful for Arrupe, who encouraged all Jesuits to identify themselves "with the body as a whole."

Arrupe, who had the highest regard for the papacy, incurred Pope Paul's anger over the question of removing inequalities of class among brothers and priests with solemn or with simple vows. This matter, widely desired in the Society, arose in the 32nd General Congregation. Delegates were unaware of Vatican disapproval. Arrupe was summoned to the Pope's presence, accused of disobedience, and sent back to the assembly profoundly shaken.

Arrupe's leadership appeared most powerfully in his convening of the 32nd General Congregation (1974-1975) to articulate afresh the Jesuit mission "to the service of the faith and the promotion of justice...for the building of a world at once more human and more divine." He encouraged varied apostolates within this mission. To him belongs the phrase "men and women for others" as the goal of Jesuit education.

The 32nd Congregation addressed the world's unjust systems from the stance of serving the faith to which "the promotion of justice is indispensable" (Decree 4). Arrupe remembered that this challenge had sparked anger among some Jesuit alumni whom he had addressed in Valencia in 1973. Their accusations and withdrawal of support were in his mind when he told the Congregation, "The justice of the Gospel should be preached through the cross and from the cross."

Through difficult years he defended his men when they took Decree 4 seriously. Some used Liberation Theology to understand the Gospel from the perspective of the oppressed. The Vatican began to hear complaints from Latin American bishops and oligarchs.

Arrupe's scope was global. He participated in bishops' conferences, notably in the prophetic meetings at Medellin (1968) and Puebla (1979). He was elected and reelected president of the international Union of Superiors General.

After fourteen years in office, Arrupe hoped to resign. Pope John Paul II asked him to postpone the discussion of his resignation. An attempt on the Pope's life in 1981 deferred the topic indefinitely.

Meanwhile, Father General Arrupe suffered a stroke on August 7, 1981. He named Vincent O'Keefe Vicar-general to act during his incapacitation and to plan for the future. Instead, there came a stroke to Arrupe's heart: Pope John Paul appointed his own delegate, Paolo Dezza, to head the Society and to prepare for a new election.

The 33rd General Congregation accepted Arrupe's resignation on September 13, 1983, giving him a thunderous acclamation. Arrupe kissed Dezza's hand. The Congregation then elected Peter-Hans Kolvenbach.

Bit by bit, illness claimed the strength of a once-vital body and mind. Brother Rafael Bandera was Arrupe's faithful nurse, Ignacio Echaniz his chaplain. Miguel Lamet interviewed Arrupe for a biography and found that his mind was clearest when his emotions were involved. He was often sad. "I wait, I wait. For me nothing, nothing. God above, the Heart of the Lord, on this poor one."

Another stroke in November 1987 drove the invalid further into silence. He had once written, "Often we set out to seek the Lord where we want him to be and not in the place where he is and awaits us. But, little by little, the Jesuit learns to recognize the Cross in its many varied forms, behind which the Lord is hidden."

"To throw yourself into the arms of the Lord...." This Jesuit reached his goal on February 5, 1991.

In recognition of his holiness, Pedro Arrupe is titled a Servant of God.

■ The Heart of Ignatius on the Mind of Arrupe *by Robert Gilroy, S.J. (By permission of the artist)*

Martyrs of Solidarity

"If we follow Christ, persecution will come." – Pedro Arrupe

Rutilio Grande (1928-1977)

Central America inherited wide class divisions from its colonial past. National independence under dictators did not change the oppression of the campesinos. They labored for meager wages on large plantations and eked out a living on rented patches of land. Landowners' militias maintained this social disorder by cruel violence. The Church was long identified with the status quo and with the privileged class—in El Salvador, the Fourteen Families.

At Medellin, Mexico, in 1968, the Latin American bishops called for social transformation.

Rutilio Grande is most widely known for the twelve bullets that riddled his body on March 12, 1977. Those who understand his martyrdom reflect on his team-based evangelization, proclaiming the liberating power of the Gospel. Few know the tormented, unsure young man who almost backed out of his ordination.

A promising youngster, Archbishop Luis Chavez of San Salvador must have thought, when he met the boy Rutilio on a pastoral visit to El Paisnal. They began to correspond. At twelve Rutilio wrote of his desire to become a priest. At thirteen he began studies in the diocesan seminary, staffed by Jesuits. After high school he joined the Society. He made his novitiate in Venezuela and studied humanities and science in Ecuador.

Rutilio gave himself fully. His generosity found its proper outlet in action. Teaching gave him respite from study, first at Xavier High School in Panama and then in San Salvador. He enjoyed the students and the practical activities.

His own studies could be postponed but not omitted. In 1953 he began three years of philosophy and four of theology in Oña, Spain. For Rutilio the world of ideas and introspection was a nightmare. The more he wrestled in it, the

Three roadside crosses mark the site where Rutilio Grande was martyred, along with Don Manuel Solórzano and Nelson Rutilio Lemus The replacement crossbar testifies to the work of vandals (Photo courtesy of Ken Overberg, S.J.)

more inadequate he felt. He was a perfectionist, and the more he looked at himself, the closer he came to despair.

"Wrenching doubts," he wrote later, came with "pounding insistence" as the date of ordination approached in July 1959. Despite the encouragement of his superiors, he felt unworthy. The new Father Grande went through the ceremonies afraid that the very act of being ordained might have been sinful. His health was shattered.

Teaching once again helped, but tertianship in 1962 promised a relapse into painful introspection. Then a light shone into his life: Lumen Vitae, the international catechetical institute in Brussels, Belgium. The Second Vatican Council was underway, and Lumen Vitae breathed the "fresh air" for which Pope John XXIII had opened the Church's windows. Rutilio began to understand that God did not ask him to be worthy. His mission was not to become perfect but to accept and to extend to others God's healing love.

This was his turning point: he trained his eyes on God, not on himself. "I promise not to be a perfectionist again.... I put all my trust in Jesus; he is the only thing that remains."

The man who returned to El Salvador in 1964 had replaced doubt with trust, depression with energy. Pastoral training became his mission. He was preparing future priests for practical ministry among the campesinos—and challenging the Church's coziness with the ruling class. Archbishop Chavez involved him in preparations for a bishops' conference in 1970. The words still ring boldly: "From sterile immobility...let us leap out and run the risk and the adventure of living a life of fidelity!" Preaching on the feast of the Transfiguration, in the cathedral in the presence of the president, Grande called for the transfiguration of the nation according to *Jesús Salvador*, "history's preëminent revolutionary," who "enfleshed himself as one of our peasants.... Can we call ourselves his followers and not do the same?"

Certain bishops were not happy! Losing their trust, Grande resigned from the seminary staff. This painful but providential step took him to a pastoral course in Ecuador.

Appointed to direct the Vice-Province's pastoral work, Grande developed a plan of team evangelization and immersion in peasant life. He and three other Jesuits were sent to Aguilares (near El Paisnal) in 1973 for a pilot project.

Among their 30,000 parishioners were campesinos (the vast majority) and landowners, overseers and militias. The ministry began with a fifteen-day mission given in twenty-five local centers. The Gospel was the starting point, with

João de Deus Gonçalves Kamtedza (1930-1985)

A man of heart, João de Deus Gonçalves Kamtedza could not leave his people to face Mozambique's violence unsupported.

Father Kamtedza's buoyant charm energized evangelization and development work in his home province of Tete. He lifted the spirits of Catholics in the Chapotera Mission. His enthusiasm inspired other Jesuits to follow a missionary vocation. "I cannot imagine [the district] without Father João de Deus, who moved about encouraging everyone to faith and hope," his superior would later write of him.

Civil war was raining terror on the population. The "incredible scarcity and hunger, the granaries burnt..." broke Kamtedza's heart, he said. He described robberies, beatings and murderous raids on villages.

Only the missionaries dared to protest. In June and July 1985, several Jesuits were kidnapped from other missions. Kamtedza and Silvio Alves Moreira (a Portuguese who had arrived that year) were advised to leave Chapotera. They chose to stay.

Late on October 29, a car approached the mission. Gunshots were heard. On November 4, among the bushes, searchers found the bodies of Kamtedza and Silvio, pierced by bullets and bayonets.

the people reflecting on the message and applying it to their own lives. Natural leaders emerged, chosen by their neighbors as "delegates of the Word." With further training, they would be faith-leaders for their communities.

The pastoral work was essentially religious, but it had social consequences. Gradually the campesinos understood their dignity; they began to demand just wages. They organized a strike at La Cabaña plantation. Landowners and their militias labeled the pastors, especially Grande, "subversives, Communists." Several pastoral workers were tortured. The president-elect promised in early 1977 to cleanse the country of Jesuits.

■ *A shrine has replaced the crosses where Grande and his companions died .*
(Photo courtesy of Brennan Hill)

Christophe Munzihirwa Mwene Ngabo (1926-1996)

Two million ethnic Hutus from Rwanda, fleeing genocide by ethnic Tutsis, poured over the border into Zaire (now Democratic Republic of Congo) in 1994. Violence became pandemic. In October 1996, Zaire's army was burning Bukavu, while Rwanda's army bore down on the city.

"Pray much for me," Christophe Munzihirwa begged his friends, "for I see that I am walking to my death." Bukavu's new archbishop was rushing home from the African Synod in Rome as a tidal wave of Hutu refugees engulfed Zaire. He preached, "Let us have a welcoming attitude to all; we shall be the richer."

A Shi born near Lake Kivu, Munzihirwa condemned the aggression of both sides. This "mzee" (wise old man) was a leader—as intellectual, as Jesuit Provincial, as apostolic administrator and now as archbishop. In 1971, when seminarians were drafted, he enlisted. In 1995, he obtained the release of arrested solidarity workers by threatening to camp outside their prison. Now Munzihirwa gathered a civilian Defense Committee; he challenged military officials to stem the violence; he denounced it to the international community—"the voice of the people," said a coworker.

"There are things that can be seen only with eyes that have cried," Munzihirwa often repeated.

The archbishop visited his frightened flock, though soldiers were confiscating vehicles at gunpoint. Late on October 29, Munzihirwa and Boni, faithful employee of the Jesuits' Alfijiri School, headed home. A soldier rode with them for protection.

The inevitable hail of bullets stopped their car in Nyawere Square. The military escort was gunned down immediately. Munzihirwa stepped out of the car, hoping Boni would be spared.. Holding his crucifix, he crossed the road toward the attackers. They shoved him, face first, against a utility pole and Boni against a tree. Munzihirwa gripped his white rosary. A single bullet to the back of the head dispatched the shepherd. Another sent Boni with him.

When a neighboring pastor was expelled from the country, Grande preached on the country's "hour of martyrdom. It has become practically illegal to be a genuine Christian...." He concluded that, should Jesus walk the roads of El Salvador, "he would be accused as a rebel, a trouble-maker."

Grande opened the novena before the feast of St. Joseph in El Paisnal. A villager, Marciano Estrada, slit the canvas on the priest's Jeep Safari in the form of a cross placed like a target at the level of the driver's head. The next day, March 12, Estrada's brother and some strangers cruised along the road between Aguilares and El Paisnal, in a blue car with United States license plates. Benito Estrada chose a place for ambush.

The Jeep left Aguilares in the late afternoon to return to El Paisnal for devotions. Rutilio Grande was driving. His passengers were 72-year-old Don Manuel Solórzano, the parish watchman, and 15-year-old Nelson Rutilio Lemus, the bell-ringer. Along the road they picked up three children.

A truck came into view behind them. At the chosen place, Benito Estrada stepped into the road and signaled to the men with him. Mantzer rifles, police-issue, rose from their sides. The passengers froze.

As the bullets struck him, Grande lost control of the Jeep, which turned on its left side, the wheels still rotating. The two men died at once. A single bullet to the forehead dispatched the boy. The children scrambled out and ran home, bloody and screaming.

Three simple coffins side by side in the cathedral attested to solidarity, in martyrdom as in life. The new Archbishop, Oscar Romero, presided. The martyrs' blood awakened his conscience; he would share their mission and their triumphant death.

■ *The people of El Paisnal created this mural honoring native son Rutilio Grande (left) and Archbishop Oscar Romero as "Prophets of Liberation," amid their people. (Photo courtesy of Ken Overberg, S.J.)*

Martyrs of the Central American University (d. November 16, 1989)

Truth.

The Jesuits had consecrated the Central American University (UCA) in San Salvador to truth.

The internationally esteemed philosopher-theologian Ignacio Ellacuría presided over UCA's transformation into an agent of social change. "A university inspired by Christian faith," he explained, "focuses all of its university activity...from the illuminating perspective of what a preferential option for the poor means." He and colleagues Ignacio Martín-Baró, Segundo Montes and Jon Sobrino shed the light of that analysis on El Salvador's economy, health, education, agriculture, finances and oppressive political-military structures. The Jesuits revered and collaborated with Archbishop Oscar Romero, martyred in 1980.

UCA's truths were rewarded with bombs and lies: "The Jesuit Communists foment violence.... UCA is a hotbed of leadership for guerilla rebels."

After the guerillas—Farabundo Marti para la Liberación Nacional (FMLN)—attacked the capital on November 11, 1989, government-controlled radio stations broadcast demands for the deaths of the Jesuits and others. Soldiers searched UCA and found Ellacuría just back from Spain; Sobrino was in Thailand. During a curfew on November 15, the Jesuits' cook, Julia Elba Ramos, and her daughter Celina stayed in the UCA compound overnight for safety.

Thirty-five soldiers broke in about 1 a.m. Montes and Ellacuría, in nightclothes, opened the doors. Martín-Baró, Juan Ramón Moreno and Amando López were dragged from their rooms. All were forced to lie face-down in the garden. There a soldier with an AK47 blew out their brains. The elderly Salvadorean Father Joaquin López y López emerged from his room and was dispatched by a bullet.

Meanwhile, the women were discovered, the mother shielding her daughter with her own body. Both were shot dead.

The government's next lie was that the FMLN had assassinated the Jesuits. The truth—martyrdom for justice' sake—emerged largely through the Society's persistent quest.

"These martyrs do not want revenge.... What they want is peace and justice for El Salvador...." – Jon Sobrino, S.J.

IGNACIO ELLACURÍA, S.J.
9 NOVEMBER 1930 – 16 NOVEMBER 1989

IGNACIO MARTÍN BARÓ, S.J.
7 NOVEMBER 1942 – 16 NOVEMBER 1989

SEGUNDO MONTES MOZO, S.J.
15 MAY 1933 – 16 NOV. 1989

Roses now grow where martyrs' blood once soaked into the soil: garden of Central American University, with the Oscar Romero Pastoral Center to the right. The husband of Celia Ramos planted yellow roses in memory of his wife and daughter, red roses in memory of the Jesuits. (Photo courtesy of Ken Overberg, S.J.)

Chapter VII

Men on a Mission in the 21st Century

*"As [The Risen Lord] is present, so we too want to be present,
in solidarity and compassion, where the human family is most damaged....
Because we are companions of Jesus, our identity is inseparable from our mission....
Our Jesuit mission touches something fundamental in the human heart:
the desire to find God in a world scarred by sin,
and then to live by his Gospel in all its implications.
...the Gospel, having been brought to the very center of a society,
touches its structural, cultural, and religious aspects with its light."*
(34th General Congregation (1995)

Men on a mission!
When? In a new millennium.
Where? Around the globe. In inter-provincial collaboration.
How? As companions of Jesus. With friends in the Lord, with fellow Christians,
with sisters and brothers in the great human family. As contemplatives in action.
Why? For the greater glory of God. To help souls. In the service of faith.
In the promotion of justice.

Peter-Hans Kolvenbach

*Father General
Peter-Hans Kolvenbach
visits with a Maya chief
in Chizami, India.
(Courtesy of Society
of Jesus Office of Press
and Information)*

Men on a Mission
in the 21st Century

About 2,500,000 students in 68 countries attend almost 3500 Jesuit educational institutions. Father General Peter-Hans Kolvenbach's criterion for Jesuit universities fits them all: "The real measure...lies in who our students become...and the adult Christian responsibility they will exercise in future towards their neighbor and their world." Besides higher, secondary and primary education, there are Jesuit technical and professional schools. Over 2500 Fe y Alegría schools promote popular education and empowerment in Latin America's most impoverished sectors.

"Forming men and women for others, in imitation of Christ, the Man for others" (Arrupe), Jesuit schools strive to be a leaven of transformation in the culture. Founded on faith, they operate from an Ignatian worldview and appreciation of the person that stress freedom, discernment and intellectual and affective development in forming leaders.

Lay men and women share the mission of Jesuit education in increasing numbers, co-responsible in an educational community of mission.

On the frontiers of thought, Jesuit scholars and specialists expand understanding and deepen reflection. Here too faith and justice are priorities, for example, in selecting areas for research.

Printing was the new medium of communication in the Society's earliest days, and Jesuits have always published books and periodicals. Later they entered radio (including the Vatican radio) and television. Jesuit missionaries now navigate the World Wide Web, offering spiritual and educational resources.

Jesuits are found in urban social centers, among immigrants and in refugee camps. They foster economic and ecological development. Their work stretches from analyzing systems of

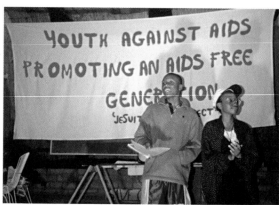

■ *The Jesuit AIDS Network engages youths such as these in addressing the AIDS pandemic on physical, social, cultural and spiritual levels. (Yearbook S.J. 2002, courtesy of Society of Jesus Office of Press and Information)*

■ *The team at Ignatiushuis, a Catholic spirituality center at the heart of Amsterdam, offers a wide range of courses, meditation meetings, training for lay parish workers, and other programs in an ecumenical spirit. (Yearbook S.J. 2003, courtesy of Society of Jesus Office of Press and Information)*

oppression to caring for the sick. Faith and Justice networks and forums link analysis with action. Gospel-based love and solidarity point these efforts toward "a world at once more human and more divine" (32nd General Congregation).

Jesuit pastors are most likely to be found in poor rural and urban parishes. Besides the core sacramental and preaching ministries, the Society fosters lay spirituality, for example by developing fresh ways for parishioners to benefit from the Spiritual Exercises.

The Exercises lay the foundations of Jesuit retreat houses and spirituality centers. Ignatian formation programs equip lay men and women to lead others in spiritual ministry.

Pastoral and spiritual apostolates are essential to the promotion not only of faith but of justice because, in the words of Kolvenbach, "Paradoxically, the problem is of a spiritual nature rather than of a purely economical one: the solution lies in the transformation of the heart, without which the poor shall become poorer while the rich shall continue increasing their wealth."

■ *Daily Prayer Online is a cyberspace ministry of Australian Jesuits, offering prayer resources and responses to questions about spiritual concerns (Webpage image courtesy of Church Resources)*

The arts engage Jesuits as they reach for truth and touch the spirit. Finding God in creation, finding themselves, finding hope for a more human world, artists share the fruits of their exploration.

Peter-Hans Kolvenbach (b. 1928)

When young Peter-Hans Kolvenbach studied modern languages at the Jesuit secondary school in Nijmegen, the Netherlands, he could not have envisioned his global ministry. As the Society's 29th Father General, he has visited 112 countries.

Peter-Hans entered the novitiate in 1948 and was ordained to the priesthood in 1961. After theological and linguistic studies at St. Joseph University in Beirut, Lebanon, and elsewhere, he taught both general and oriental linguistics in Paris and Beirut (1963-1981). Father Kolvenbach's experience in Lebanon, where he was also Provincial superior, led to his appointment as rector of the Pontifical Oriental Institute in Rome in 1981.

The 33rd General Congregation elected Kolvenbach in 1983 to succeed Pedro Arrupe. Arrupe's term had been cut off by illness and by the appointment of a papal delegate. To Kolvenbach fell the delicate task of rebuilding damaged relationships with the Vatican. His multi-cultural understanding and diplomatic sensitivity have served the Society and the Church well.

In February 2006, Kolvenbach announced plans for a 35th General Congregation for January 2007, to elect his successor.

■ *(Courtesy of Society of Jesus Office of Press and Information)*

Inter-religious dialogue is a new Jesuit mission, called for by Pope John Paul II, though models go far back in the Society's history. Jesuits also respond to the challenges of atheism, which Pope Paul VI asked the Society to address. Others strive for Christian unity through ecumenical dialogue. Besides the specialists, many welcome the "dialogue of daily life" (Kolvenbach) in personal encounters that build respect and mutual understanding.

Jesuits lead the Apostleship of Prayer for intentions requested by the Pope. Millions unite in prayer, generating global awareness and spiritual energy for the Church universal.

Lay participants in Christian Life Communities (CLC) benefit from the spiritual guidance of Jesuit assistants. The sodality movement, of which CLC is a form, has its roots in the early Society.

■ *In the Beqaa Valley in Lebanon, Jesuits and Sacred Heart sisters collaborate in running St. Elias Jesuit Elementary School in Talabaya. These students and their teachers come from communities of both Christians and Muslims who are economically poor. (Photo by Moussa Faddoul, S.J.)*

■ *Christian Life Communities offer life and hope to many young men and women in Lebanon's Beqaa Valley. Here CLC member Nicola Saliba prays during a night meditation on Light at Our Lady of Consolata Retreat Centre in Tanayel. (Photo by Moussa Faddoul, S.J.)*

■ *Albert Alejo, S.J., hosts a reflection segment on Magandang Umaga Pilipinas (Good Morning Philippines) a daily TV show. This episode features the theme, "Blessed are the creative in the midst of crisis." (Photo courtesy of Jesuit Communications Foundation, Inc., Manila, producer of the TV segment)*

■ *Fr. Amalraj Chinnappan, a Jesuit from India's Madurai Province, stands with Liberian children in 2004. The director of the Jesuit Refugee Service in Liberia, he had previously worked among Sri Lankans fleeing to India and had served as the JRS regional director for South Asia. (Photo courtesy of* Company *magazine)*

A Closing Word

For the better part of five centuries, Ignatius Loyola's experience of God—present, calling, loving—has inspired the men who have followed him. Each Jesuit walks his own spiritual journey as a companion of Jesus. The Society's mission to serve God and help souls has taken different forms in different centuries. Jesuits enter the twenty-first century serving faith and promoting justice.

Take, Lord, and receive all my liberty,
my memory, my understanding, and my entire will,
all that I have and possess.
Thou hast given all to me.
To thee, O Lord, I return it.
All is Thine, dispose of it wholly according to Thy will.
Give me Thy love and Thy grace,
for this is sufficient for me.

Ignatius Loyola,
The Spiritual Exercises

(Painting by José de Ribera,
Courtesy of the Institute of Jesuit Sources)

Jesuits Canonized and Beatified

Saints

Andlauer, Modeste
Arrowsmith, Edmund
Bellarmine, Robert
Berchmans, John
Bobola, Andrew
Borgia, Francis
Brébeuf, John de
Briant, Alexander
Brito, John de
Campion, Edmund
Canisius, Peter
Castillo, John del
Chabanel, Noel
Claver, Peter
Daniel, Anthony
Denn, Paul
Evans, Philip

Garnet, Thomas
Garnier, Charles
Geronimo, Francis de
Gonzaga, Aloysius
Gonzalez de Santa Cruz, Roch
Goto, John de
Goupil, René
Grodziecki, Melchior
Hurtado Cruchaga, Alberto
Isoré, Rémy
Jogues, Isaac
Kisai, James
Kostka, Stanislaus
La Colombière, Claude
La Lande, John de
Lalemant, Gabriel
Lewis, David

Loyola, Ignatius
Mangin, Leo Ignatius
Miki, Paul
Morse, Henry
Ogilvie, John
Owen, Nicholas
Pignatelli, Joseph
Pongrácz, Stephen
Realino, Bernardino
Regis, John Francis
Rodríguez, Alphonsus (d. 1617)
Rodríguez, Alphonsus (d. 1628)
Rubio Peralta, Joseph Mary
Southwell, Robert
Walpole, Henry
Xavier, Francis

Blessed

Acquaviva, Rudolph
Akahoshi, Thomas
Alvarez, Francis
Alvarez, Gaspar
Alvarez, Manuel
Anchieta, José de
Andrade, James de
Andrieux, René
Aranha, Francis
Ashley, Ralph
Azevedo, Ignatius de & Companions
Baena, Alphonsus de
Baldinucci, Anthony
Balmain, Francis
Basté Basté, Narcissus
Benoît-Vourlat, John
Bérauld du Pérou, Charles
Berno, Peter

Berthieu, Jacques
Beyzym, John
Bonnaud, James
Borralho Méndez, Alvaro
Bori Puig, Paul
Caldeira, Mark
Carbonell Sempere, Constantine
Carvalho, James
Carvalho, Michael
Castro, Benedict de
Cayx-Dumas, Claude
Charton de Millou, John
Chugoku, John
Collins, Dominic
Corby, Ralph
Cordier, John Nicholas
Cornelius, John
Correia, Anthony

Correia, Louis
Costa, Simon da
Costanzo, Camillus
Cottam, Thomas
De Angelis, Jerome
Delfaud, William
Delgado, Alexis
Dinis, Nicholas
Escribano, Gregory
Faber, Peter
Fenwick, John
Fernándes, Ambrose
Fernándes, Anthony
Fernándes, Dominic
Fernándes, John I
Fernándes, John II
Fernándes, Manuel
Ferreres Boluda, John Baptist

Blessed

Filcock, Roger
Fontoura, Peter
Francisco, Anthony
Friteyre-Durvé, James
Fujishima, Dennis
Fusai, Gonzalo
Gagnières des Granges, Francis
Gaius
Gárate, Francis
Gavan, John
Gelabert Amer, Peter
Gonçalves, Andrew
Grimaltos Monllor, Raymond
Guérin de Rocher, Peter
Guérin de Rocher, Robert
Harcourt, William
Hernández Morató, Darius
Henriques, Gonçalo
Herque du Roule, Elias
Holland, Thomas
Imbert, Joseph
Ireland, William
Ishida, Anthony
John (?)
Kaun, Vincent
Kawara, Louis
Kimura, Leonard
Kimura, Sebastian
Kinsuke, Paul
Kisaku, John
Kyuni, Anthony

Lanfant, Alexander
Laporte, Claude
Le Bous de Villenueve, Mathurin
Le Gué, Charles
Le Livec, Francis
Le Rousseau de Rosancoat, Vincent
Lópes, Simon
Machado, John Baptist
Magalhães, Francis de
Maunoir, Julian
Mayer, Rupert
Mayorga, John de
Mimoso Pires, James
Middleton, Robert
Nakashima, Michael
Navarro, Peter Paul
Nelson, John
Nunes, Peter
Oldcorne, Edward
Onizuka, Sandaju Peter
Ota, Augustine
Pacheco, Alphonsus
Pacheco, Francis
Pacheco, Manuel
Page, Francis
Pérez Godoy, Francis
Pro Juárez, Miguel Augustín
Ribeiro, Bras
Rinscei, Peter
Rodrigues, Louis
Rodrigues, Manuel

Sadamatsu, Caspar
Salès, James
Sales Genovés, Vincent
Sampo, Peter
Sánchez, Ferdinand
San Martin, John de
San Vitores, James Louis de
Saultemouche, William
Seconds, John
Shumpo, Michael
Simón Colomina, Alfred
Sitjar Fortía, Thomas
Soares, Anthony
Spinola, Charles
Tarrats Comaposada, Joseph
Thomas-Bonnotte, Louis
Torres, Balthasar de
Tozo, Michael
Tsuji, Thomas
Turner, Anthony
Variehle-Duteil, Francis
Vaz, Amaro
Verron, Nicholas Marie
Whitbread, Thomas
Woodhouse, Thomas
Wright, Peter
Yempo, Simon
Zafra, John de
Zola, John Baptist
Zuraire, Stephen

■ *St. Dominic Collins (left) as cavalry officer, (right) tending the sick, (center) martyred at Youghal, County Cork, Ireland in 1602. (Reproduced courtesy of the Irish Province of the Society of Jesus)*

Bibliography
of Works Consulted

Allen, John L., Jr. "Faith, Hope and Heroes," *National Catholic Reporter* (Feb. 23, 2001), 13-17.

Arrupe, Pedro, S.J. *One Jesuit's Spiritual Journey: Autobiographical Conversations with Jean-Claude Dietsch, S.J.*, trans. Ruth Bradley. St. Louis, Missouri: The Institute of Jesuit Sources, 1986.

Arrupe, Pedro, S.J. *Selected Letters and Addresses, Vols. 1, 2, 3*, ed. Jerome Aixala, S.J. St. Louis, Missouri: The Institute of Jesuit Sources, 1979-1981.

Bailey, Gauvin Alexander. *Art on the Jesuit Missions in Asia and Latin America, 1542-1773*. Toronto: University of Toronto Press, 1999.

Bangert, William V., S.J. *A History of the Society of Jesus*. St. Louis, Missouri: The Institute of Jesuit Sources, 1972.

Barry, William A., S.J., and Robert G. Doherty, S.J. *Contemplatives in Action: The Jesuit Way*. New York: Paulist Press, 2002.

Bishop, George. *Pedro Arrupe, S.J.: Twenty-eighth General of the Society of Jesus*. Gujarat: Gujarat Sahitya Prakash, India, 2000.

Brackley, Dean, S.J. "Higher Standards," *America* (February 6, 2006), 9-13.

Brodrick, James, S.J. *The Progress of the Jesuits (1556-79)*, originally published in 1940. Chicago: Loyola University Press, 1986.

Brodrick, James, S.J. *Saint Francis Xavier*. New York: The Wicklow Press, 1952.

Burke, Marcus B. *Jesuit Art and Iconography 1550-1800: Introductory Essay and Exhibition Catalogue*. Jersey City, New Jersey: St. Peter's College Art Gallery, 1993.

Caraman, Philip. *Ignatius Loyola: A Biography of the Founder of the Jesuits*. San Francisco: Harper & Row, Publishers, 1990.

Caraman, Philip. *The Lost Paradise: The Jesuit Republic in South America*. New York: The Seabury Press, 1976.

Carriker, Robert C. *Father Peter John De Smet: Jesuit in the West*, Vol. 9 in *The Oklahoma Western Biographies Series*. Norman, Oklahoma: University of Oklahoma Press, 1995.

Chipps Smith, Jeffrey. *Sensuous Worship: Jesuits and the Art of the Early Catholic Reformation in Germany*. Princeton, New Jersey: Princeton University Press, 2002.

Ciszek, Walter, S.J., with Daniel L. Flaherty, S.J. *He Leadeth Me*, originally published by Doubleday and Company, Inc., 1973, reprinted in San Francisco: Ignatius Press, 1995.

Ciszek, Walter, S.J., with Daniel L. Flaherty, S.J. *With God in Russia*. New York: The America Press, 1964.

Cordara, Giulio Cesare. *On the Suppression of the Jesuits: A Contemporary Account*, trans. and notes by John P. Murphy. Chicago: Loyola Press, 1999.

Corley, Francis J., S.J., and Robert J. Willmes, S.J. *Wings of Eagles: The Jesuit Saints and Blessed*. Milwaukee: The Bruce Publishing Company, 1941.

Curran, Robert Emmett. *The Bicentennial History of Georgetown University*, Vol. I: From Academy to University, 1789-1889. Washington, D.C.: Georgetown University Press, 1993.

Diccionario Histórico de la Compañia de Jesús: Biográfico-Temático, 4 vols., Charles E. O'Neill, S.J., and Joaquin M.ª Domínguez, S.J., Directors. Rome: Institutum Historicum, S.I., 2001.

Documents of the 31st and 32nd General Congregations of the Society of Jesus: An English Translation of the Official Latin Texts of the Congregations and of the Accompanying Papal Documents. St. Louis, Missouri: Institute of Jesuit Sources, 1977.

Documents of the 34th General Congregation of the Society of Jesus, ed. John L. McCarthy, S.J. St. Louis, Missouri: Institute of Jesuit Sources, 1996.

Durkin, Joseph T., S.J. *Georgetown University: First in the Nation's History*. Garden City, N.J.: Doubleday and Co., 1964.

Egan, Harvey D., S.J. Karl Rahner: *The Mystic of Everyday Life*. New York: Crossroad Publishing Company, 1998.

Echaniz, Ignacio, S.J. *Passion and Glory: A Flesh-and-blood history of the Society of Jesus*, 4 vols. Gujarat Sahitya Prakash: Anand, Gujarat, India, 1999.

Fabel, Arthur and Donald St. John, eds. *Teilhard in the 21st Century: The Emerging Spirit of Earth*. Maryknoll, New York: Orbis Books, 2003.

Hanley, D.A., P.A. Blessed Joseph Pignatelli: *A Great Leader in a Great Crisis*. Cincinnati: Benziger Brothers, 1937.

Hopkins, Gerard Manley. *Poems and Prose*, ed. W. H. Gardner. Harmondsworth, Middlesex, England: Penguin Books, 1953.

Instituto de Estudios Centroamericanos and El Rescate. *The Jesuit Assassinations: The Writings of Ellacuría, Martín-Baró and Segundo Montes, with a Chronology of the Investigation (November 11, 1989 – October 22, 1990)*. Kansas City: Sheed and Ward, 1990.

The Jesuits and the Arts 1540-1773, ed. John W. O'Malley, S.J. and Gauvin Alexander Bailey. (Italian edition published under the title *Ignazio e l'arte dei Gesuiti*, ed. Giovanni Sale, S.J., 2003.) Philadelphia: Saint Joseph's University Press, 2005.

King, Ursula. *Spirit of Fire: The Life and Vision of Teilhard de Chardin*. Maryknoll, New York: Orbis Books, 1996.

King, Thomas M. "A Holy Man and Lover of the World: The Spirituality of Teilhard de Chardin," *America* (March 28, 2005), 7-10.

Lacouture, Jean. *Jesuits: A Multibiography*, trans. Jeremy Leggatt. Washington, D.C. Counterpoint, 1995.

Leturia, Pedro, S.J. *Iñigo de Loyola*, trans. Aloysius J. Owen, S.J. Syracuse, New York: Le Moyne College Press, 1949.

Loyola, Ignatius. *The Spiritual Autobiography of St. Ignatius Loyola with Related Documents*, trans. Joseph F. O'Callaghan; ed. with introduction and notes John C. Olin. New York: Harper and Row, 1974.

Loyola, Ignatius. *The Spiritual Exercises of St. Ignatius*, ed. Louis J. Puhl, S.J. Chicago: Loyola University Press, 1951.

Lucas, Thomas M., S.J. *Landmarking: City, Church and Jesuit Urban Strategy*. Chicago: Loyola Press, 1997.

Lucas, Thomas M., S.J. "Virtual Vessels, Mystical Signs: Contemplating Mary's Images in the Jesuit Tradition," *Studies in the Spirituality of Jesuits* (November 2003), 1-46.

MacDonnell, Joseph F., S.J. *Jesuit Family Album: Sketches of Chivalry from the Early Society*. Fairfield, Connecticut: Clavius Group, 1997.

Marquette, Jacques. *Voyages of Marquette in The Jesuit Relations*, 59. Ann Arbor, Michigan: University Microfilms, Inc., 1966.

McCarty, Doran. *Teilhard de Chardin*, in series *Makers of the Modern Theological Mind*, ed. Bob E. Patterson. Waco, Texas: Word Books, 1976.

McGloin, John Bernard, S.J. *Eloquent Indian: The Life of James Bouchard, California Jesuit*. Stanford, California: Stanford University Press, 1949.

McNaspy, C.J., S.J. *Lost Cities of Paraguay: Art and Architecture of the Jesuit Reductions 1607-1767*. Photographs by J. M. Blanch, S.J. Chicago: Loyola University Press, 1982.

Meissner, W.W., S.J. *Ignatius of Loyola: The Psychology of a Saint*. New Haven, Connecticut: Yale University Press, 1992.

Norman, Mrs. George. *God's Jester: The Story of the Life and Martyrdom of Father Michael Pro, S.J.* New York: Benziger Brothers, 1930.

O'Malley, John W., S.J. *The First Jesuits*. Cambridge, Massachusetts: Harvard University Press, 1993.

O'Malley, John W., S.J. "Introduction," for "*Ratio Studiorum*: Jesuit Education, 1548-1773," an exhibit celebrating the 400th anniversary of the first promulgation of the *Ratio Studiorum.* Boston: Boston College John J. Burns Library, 1999.

O'Malley, William J., S.J. *The Voice of Blood: Five Christian Martyrs of Our Time.* Maryknoll, New York: Orbis Books, 1980.

O'Toole, James M. *Passing for White: Race, Religion, and the Healy Family, 1820-1920.* Amherst: University of Massachusetts Press, 2002.

Polzer, Charles, S.J. "Padre on Horseback: To Obscurity and Back, toward the Beatification of Eusebio Kino, S.J.," *Company* (Summer 2002), 7-11.

Rahner, Karl, S.J. *Faith in a Wintry Season: Conversations and Interviews with Karl Rahner in the Last Years of His Life,* ed. Paul Imhof and Hubert Biallowons, trans. ed. by Harvey D. Egan. New York: Crossroad Publishing Company, 1990.

Reiter, Frederick J. *They Built Utopia: (The Jesuit Missions in Paraguay) 1610-1768.* Potomac, Maryland: Scripta Humanistica, 1995. N. B. especially P. Pablo Hernández, "Organización social de las doctrinas Guaranticas de la Compañia de Jesús.", p. viii

Rhodes, Alexander de, S.J. *Rhodes of Viet Nam: The Travels and Missions of Father Alexander de Rhodes in China and Other Kingdoms of the Orient,* trans. Solange Hertz. Westminster, Maryland: The Newman Press, 1966.

Ricci, Matthew, S.J. *China in the Sixteenth Century: The Journals of Matthew Ricci: 1583-1610,* trans. Louis J. Gallagher, S.J. New York: Random House, 1953.

Royer, Fanchón. *Padre Pro.* New York: P.J. Kenedy & Sons, 1954.

Sartre, S. E. Victor, S.J. *Il martirio del P. Berthieu S.J.* Italy: Marietti Editori Ltd., 1965.

Smith, Fay Jackson et al. *Father Kino in Arizona.* Phoenix, Arizona: Arizona Historical Foundation, 1966.

Sobrino, Jon, S.J., Ignacio Ellacuría, S.J., and others. *Companions of Jesus: The Jesuit Martyrs of El Salvador.* Maryknoll, NY: Orbis Books, 1990.

Teilhard de Chardin, Pierre, S.J. *The Divine Milieu,* trans. Bernard Wall. New York: Harper & Row, Publishers, 1960

Teilhard de Chardin, Pierre, S.J. *Letters from a Traveller.* New York: Harper & Row, Publishers, 1962.

Teilhard de Chardin, Pierre, S.J. "The Mass on the World" in *Hymn of the Universe,* trans. Gerald Vann, O.P. New York: Harper & Row, Publishers, 1965, pp. 13-47.

Teilhard de Chardin, Pierre, S.J. and Lucile Swan. *The Letters of Teilhard de Chardin and Lucile Swan,* ed. Thomas M. King, S.J. and Mary Wood Gilbert. Washington, D.C.: Georgetown University Press, 1993.

Traub, George, S.J. *Do You Speak Ignatian? A Glossary of Terms Used in Ignatian and Jesuit Circles,* fifth ed. Cincinnati, Ohio: Xavier University, 2000.

Tylenda, Joseph N., S.J. *Jesuit Saints and Martyrs: Short Biographies of the Saints, Blessed, Venerables, and Servants of God of the Society of Jesus.* Chicago: Loyola Press, 1998.

Weyand, Norman, S.J., ed. *Immortal Diamond: Studies in Gerard Manley Hopkins.* New York: Sheed and Ward, 1949.

Whitfield, Teresa. *Paying the Price: Ignacio Ellacuría and the Murdered Jesuits of El Salvador.* Philadelphia: Temple University Press, 1994.

Wright, Jonathan. *God's Soldiers: Adventure, Politics, Intrigue, and Power—A History of the Jesuits.* New York: Doubleday, 2004.

Yearbook of the Society of Jesus (published by the General Curia of the Society of Jesus) 1992, 1995, 1996, 1998, 1999, 2000, 2001, 2003, 2004.